Richard Wagner
Das Rheingold

translation and commentary
by Rudolph Sabor

For Emmi

Phaidon Press Limited
Regent's Wharf
All Saints Street
London N1 9PA

First published 1997
© 1997 Phaidon Press Limited

ISBN 0 7148 3651 6

A CIP catalogue record for this
book is available from the
British Library

Printed in Hong Kong

Frontispiece, the giants
seize Freia; illustration by
Arthur Rackham (1911)

Contents

Foreword

There is an overriding need for a new translation of Wagner's libretto to *Der Ring des Nibelungen*: the section entitled 'Translating Wagner's Ring' explains why and also specifies the particular aims of this author's version; for further discussion on the vital topic of the German *Idiom* and the individual language assigned by Wagner to each of his characters the reader is directed to the companion volume of this series.

The main section of this volume – and of the three that cover respectively *Die Walküre*, *Siegfried* and *Götterdämmerung* – consists of the German text of the *Ring*, which runs side by side with its English translation. Each leitmotif, as it appears, is indicated in the margin, which also carries the author's annotations on points of particular musical or textual interest. At the beginning of each scene is a synopsis of the plot, and a step-by-step breakdown of the action. The leitmotifs new to the scene are identified with musical quotations, and there is a brief discussion of the motifs' musical and dramatic character.

In addition to the new translation of Wagner's libretto for the first of the tetralogy, *Das Rheingold*, this volume provides a brief appreciation of the Wagnerian leitmotif, a list of the opera's characters, and notes on the orchestral transitions from scene to scene. Appendices include information on the opera's composition and performance, a selective bibliography, discography and videography, and the volume concludes with a comprehensive list of all the leitmotifs that are heard in *Das Rheingold*.

A number of people have helped me in a number of ways. Hilde Pearton, Dr Maurice Pearton and Stewart Spencer have provided comments in detail and depth. Their generous assistance far exceeds the accepted norm of collegial co-operation, and I hope the present volumes reflect their good counsel. Eric Adler has supplied valuable information about Ring performances in distant climes. The unquenchable thirst for Wagnerian enquiry and intelligence displayed by the students of my seminars on Wagner at Crayford Manor and Higham Hall has been largely responsible for the growth and scope of these five volumes. Several enlightening conversations with Wolfgang Wagner, wise guardian of the Bayreuther Festspiele, have claimed the author's attention and have contributed to smoothing his path through the complexities of the *Ring*.

Emmi Sabor has double-checked the manuscript, and I am grateful for her labour and for the serenity with which she has tolerated Richard Wagner as lodger for the best part of our lives. Lady Young, with Wagnerian seductiveness, was instrumental in persuading Phaidon Press to publish a series of books whose structural and typographical intricacies were formidable. To my editors, Edmund Forey and Ingalo Thomson, and to Hans Dieter Reichert of hdr design, I owe particular thanks for their masterminding of our joint Wagnerian safari.

Rudolph Sabor, Petts Wood, 1997

Leitmotifs: an Introduction

Appreciating the power of Wagner's system of leitmotifs adds a new dimension to our understanding of the *Ring* cycle. There are those who maintain that a leitmotif is little more than a musical visiting card which announces a character's appearance or a dramatic event. This is a fallacy. The Wagnerian leitmotif is an integral element of the *Gesamtkunstwerk*, the totality of the arts – the union of music, poetry and stage craft. It comments on the action, it recalls, it predicts, it even contradicts, occasionally, a character's words or action, but it is always *bona fide*. Leitmotifs are our accredited guides through the profundities of the *Ring*.

To alert the listener to the first appearance of a new leitmotif, Wagner generally repeats it, sometimes more than once, and he frequently prescribes an appropriate action to accompany the motif. A leitmotif undergoes many modifications in the course of the music dramas. It may be varied melodically, rhythmically or harmonically, it may be played by instruments other than those which sounded it at its first appearance. Such modifications are generally inaugurated by either musical or psychological requirements.

Wieland Wagner (1917–66), the composer's grandson, pointed out to his artists that leitmotifs were symbols, and that tracing the course of such musical symbols through the entire *Ring* would amount to a journey of discovery into the realms of depth psychology. Such a course is traced in the companion volume of this series, in the essay 'The Wagnerian Leitmotif'.

The present volumes are committed to defining and interpreting the whole set of motifs, both separately and in the context of the drama, with the aim of equipping the reader with a genuine grasp of the complexities of the work.

Translating Wagner's *Ring*

Mimi hight a manikin grim,
who in nought but greed granted me care,
to count on me, when manful I'd waxed,
in the wood to slay a worm,
which long had hidden there a hoard.

More than a hundred years ago the English-speaking world was
treated to a translation of the *Ring* by Frederick and Henrietta
Corder, husband and wife; the above is a sample of their craft.
The Corders had many successors. The most noteworthy are
Frederick Jameson in 1896, Margaret Armour in 1911, Ernest
Newman in 1912, Stewart Robb in 1960, William Mann in 1964,
Peggie Cochrane in 1965, Lionel Salter in 1966, Andrew Porter
in 1976 and Stewart Spencer in 1993.

Their translations have much to offer. I have admired and
envied many of their neat solutions to intricate problems, and I
am indebted to them all for suggesting a phrase here, a telling
word there, and for the comfortable assurance of being a suc-
cessor rather than a pioneer.

So why attempt a new translation? Because Wagner's *Ring*, in
spite of minor flaws, is a literary masterpiece, something that
none of the existing translations quite manages to convey. But
the *Ring* is not only a literary work of art. Its intricate system of
metrical patterns, its use of alliteration, its rare but telling
rhymes, its imaginative metaphors, its occasional punning, its
astonishing ambiguities, its sheer singability – all these combine to create something unique in the history of the opera
libretto: the music is in the text. The present translation aims to
provide the reader and singer with a libretto which does not
sound like a translation, but rather like the text Wagner might
have written had he been born not in Leipzig but in London.
My objectives are:
– Accuracy
– Matching German and English lines, retaining the position of
  key words
– Preserving the original metre
– Retaining alliteration and rhyme where possible
– Elucidating where Wagner is obscure
– Emulating the original by allowing each character to speak
  in his/her particular idiom

Accuracy

Confusion can arise not only from grammatical errors in translation, but also from misunderstood figures of speech; mistranslation can obscure an already complex plot.

Matching Lines and Key Words

To assist the reader, it is essential that the German text and English translation run in parallel; lines must not be transposed just to satisfy grammatical demands. Equally important is the location of key words. Where the German speaks for example of 'Schwert' (sword) or 'Liebe' (love), the word may have been given a particular melodic or instrumental setting, which would be lost if the word were displaced in translation.

Metre

It has earlier been asserted that Wagner's music is already discernible in the text. This is achieved, partly, by the astonishing variety of metre: iambs (.-), trochees (-.), anapests (..-) and spondees (--), long lines and short lines. All coexist without ever disturbing the natural flow of the text.

Alliteration and Rhyme

Wagner regarded alliteration as the textual equivalent of the musical leitmotif. In three of his prose works, *Das Kunstwerk der Zukunft*, *Eine Mitteilung an meine Freunde* and *Oper und Drama*, he stresses the importance of that method of versification which is 'another kind of rhyme'. Indeed, the German term *Stabreim* means 'spelling rhyme'. The counterpart of the *Stabreim* is the true rhyme, which Wagner uses most sparingly in the *Ring*; when he does, it heralds a matter of special importance.

Obscurity and Ambiguity

On the few occasions when Wagner's language is convoluted and the meaning becomes opaque, the translator must lend a helping hand. Wagner's libretto can also include deliberate ambiguity, which must be preserved in the translation.

Characterization

The most important aspect of Wagner's versification is the individual idiom of his characters. Wagner's characterization does not begin on the stage: it is already planned in the language of the text, where each character is given his or her own distinctive mode of expression. It is up to the translator to retrace Wagner's design.

'Poetry is what gets lost in translation,' someone once said. It is the author's sincere wish that this may not be so.

Characters of *Das Rheingold*

WOGLINDE
One of the three Rhinemaidens who guard the gold in the river. Soprano, in *Rheingold* and *Götterdämmerung*.

WELLGUNDE
One of the three Rhinemaidens who guard the gold in the river. Soprano, in *Rheingold* and *Götterdämmerung*.

FLOSSHILDE
One of the three Rhinemaidens who guard the gold in the river. More vigilant than her carefree sisters. Mezzo-soprano, in *Rheingold* and *Götterdämmerung*.

WOTAN
Chief of the gods. Husband of Fricka, father of Siegmund, Sieglinde, Brünnhilde and eight Valkyries. Rules the world from his castle, Walhall, built by Fafner and Fasolt, brother giants. Robs Alberich of gold, ring and Tarnhelm (magic cap), to pay the giants. Embroiled in false treaties and broken promises, he creates the race of the Wälsungs, i.e., Siegmund, Sieglinde, and their son Siegfried who is to rectify Wotan's judicial errors and return the ring to the Rhine. When Siegfried is killed by Hagen, Wotan commits Walhall and his fellow gods to the flames. Bass-baritone, in *Rheingold*, *Walküre* and, as Wanderer, in *Siegfried*.

FRICKA
Wotan's wife. Sister of Freia, Donner and Froh. Guardian of wedlock. Mezzo-soprano, in *Rheingold* and *Walküre*.

FREIA
Sister of Fricka, Donner and Froh. Guardian of the golden apples of youth. Soprano, in *Rheingold*.

DONNER
Brother of Fricka, Freia and Froh. God of thunder. Baritone, in *Rheingold*.

FROH

Brother of Fricka, Freia and Donner. Creates the rainbow bridge on which the gods enter into Walhall. Tenor, in *Rheingold.*

LOGE

God of fire. Ambivalent intellectual who is both ally and enemy of the gods. Tenor, in *Rheingold.*

ERDA

Earth-goddess, mother of the three Norns and of Brünnhilde. Represents knowledge of past and future. Warns Wotan to part with the cursed ring, and prophesies the eventual waning of the gods. Alto, in *Rheingold* and *Siegfried.*

ALBERICH

Father of Hagen, brother of Mime. Ruler of the Nibelungs, dwarfs living in subterranean Nibelheim. Has renounced love and forged an all-powerful ring from the stolen Rhinegold. Loses his ring to Wotan, then curses it and all future owners. Baritone, in *Rheingold, Siegfried* and *Götterdämmerung.*

MIME

Nibelung, brother of Alberich, master smith. Rears the young Siegfried, in order to obtain the Nibelung hoard. Intends to poison Siegfried, but is killed by him. Tenor, in *Rheingold* and *Siegfried.*

FAFNER

Giant, brother of Fasolt, co-builder of Walhall. Kills his brother over possession of the cursed ring. Turns himself into a dragon, with the help of the Tarnhelm, and guards the Nibelung hoard. Is killed by Siegfried. Bass, in *Rheingold* and, as Dragon, in *Siegfried.*

FASOLT

Brother of Fafner, co-builder of Walhall and the milder of the two giants. Is killed by Fafner. Bass, in *Rheingold.*

NIBELUNGS

Subterranean miners in Nibelheim, enslaved by their lord, Alberich.

The Rhinemaidens tease
Alberich; illustration by
Ludwig Burger (1876)

1
Scene

Synopsis
Leitmotifs
Libretto

Scene 1: Story

On the Bed of the Rhine

Woglinde, Wellgunde and Flosshilde, the Rhinemaidens (or Rhinedaughters) are at play, swimming and splashing about. Flosshilde warns her sisters not to neglect their duty, the guarding of the Rhinegold.

The ugly dwarf Alberich appears from below, and is enchanted by the beautiful spectacle. The Rhinemaidens tease him, pretending to find him attractive and then mocking him; Alberich pursues them furiously. The Rhinegold begins to glow and the Rhinemaidens swim joyously around it, basking in its brilliance. They inform Alberich that a ring could be forged from the gold, and that he who wore the ring would become all-powerful. They add, however, that this will never be, since the gold could be obtained only by forswearing love, and no living creature would ever do that. Alberich, maddened by the Rhinemaidens' taunts, renounces love, snatches the gold and disappears with it. The Rhinemaidens bewail their lost gold.

Stage machinery for the Rhinemaidens, Bayreuth 1876

Scene 1: Action

1. Orchestra: Beginnings
2. Rhinemaidens' games
3. Alberich appears
4. Woglinde teases Alberich
5. Wellgunde teases Alberich
6. Flosshilde teases Alberich
7. They mock him together
8. Alberich pursues them
9. Rhinegold begins to glow
10. Rhinemaidens bask in the golden glow
11. They give away its secret
12. Alberich snatches the gold and renounces love
13. Rhinemaidens panic
14. Orchestra: from the depth of the Rhine to the mountain top

Note that this first scene of *Rheingold* is mirrored by the last scene of *Götterdämmerung*:

Rheingold	*Götterdämmerung*
Alberich invades the Rhein	Alberich's son, Hagen, invades the Rhein
Alberich grabs the gold	Hagen grabs the gold
The world begins	The world ends

Scene 1: Leitmotifs

The leitmotifs new to the scene follow in chronological order, together with the page number of first appearance.

Genesis   p.22

Innocence   p.22

Alberich   p.26

Liebe-Tragik   p.32

Grief   p.34

Liebesnot   p.34

Rhinegold   p.36

Joy p.38

Ring p.40

Crisis   Transition

Commentary on the Leitmotifs

Genesis

So low is the first note, E flat, that the double basses have to tune their E strings down a semitone. Eight double basses sustain this E flat. In the fifth bar three bassoons enter on B flat. The fundamental tonic is joined by its dominant. Peace is broken into. Life has begun. Genesis.

Innocence

This motif is first heard at the very beginning of the first scene. It is based on a pentatonic (5-note) scale. Woglinde sings the motif to the words:

Weia! Waga! Woge, du Welle! Walle zur Wiege!
(Weia! Waga! Wandering waters, cradle us, rock us!)

The Innocence motif appears a few more times in the course of *Rheingold*, but will not be heard again until *Götterdämmerung*.

Alberich

Strictly speaking this is not a leitmotif, but a simple theme. It does not develop musically, but it does tell us something about Alberich's personality. The coiling, fast moving theme (played by cellos and double basses) carries sufficient menace for the Rhinemaidens to take note and beware. But they don't.

Liebe-Tragik

This descending scale segment, which is encountered in two shapes, will assume great importance in the development of the drama. Dwelling on the first note, it descends, step by weighty step. The Liebe-Tragik motif is heard when a character is aware of distressing circumstances, of impending doom, even of his own baseness, and is prepared to face such baseness, doom or distress. It always speaks of love and of the inevitability of love's sorrow. It has a tragic ring. It disregards consequences. It says, 'And yet!' On the day he died Wagner was working on an essay. His last words were 'Liebe-Tragik' (love-tragedy); then the pen slipped from his hand. Liebe-Tragik is a motto for the whole *Ring*.

Grief

Two notes only, a descending semitone. This motif will be heard whenever frustration or anguish mars human or divine endeavour. It occurs constantly throughout the *Ring*. It screams, whimpers and moans in the orchestra as it comments on the folly of man, on the agony of life.

Liebesnot

This figure has variously been named the Love, Flight or Fear motif. It symbolizes in fact a rather more complex emotion, the distress which is often caused by and fused with love. It is akin to the Liebe-Tragik motif. The German term for this aspect of the human condition is 'Liebesnot' (love's distress).

Rhinegold

This fanfare-like motif is first announced by a French horn. Its opening interval, the rising fourth, gives a strong sense of direction. We shall meet other motifs which begin with the same purposeful interval: Donner's call, the Sword, the Ride of the Valkyries, Siegfried, Hosanna, and the Assurance motif. If one wanted to classify all these musical–dramatic symbols, their heading might be Lucifer, bringer of light.

   The Rhinegold motif, incidentally, was anticipated in Carl Loewe's 'Erl King', composed when Wagner was five years old. In Goethe's text the Erl King, demon phantom of vapour, calls to the young boy, 'Come here, my child, and come with me!'

„Komm, lie - bes Kind, komm, geh mit mir!

The Erl King's call and the Rhinegold motif (both in G major) break into an existing situation and cast their peculiar spell, the one on the boy, the other on Alberich.

Joy

Another two-note motif, the symbol of joy. This is derived from the first two notes of the Innocence motif. The falling whole tone is in strong contrast to the falling semitone of the Grief motif. In the course of the *Ring* Wagner frequently presents both motifs in close juxtaposition; occasionally they are even played simultaneously. Joy and grief, says Wagner, are interrelated.

Ring

At its first appearance this motif starts on an E, coils downwards and back up again, but only as far as B, falling short of
a complete circuit. The ring, we are told, is incomplete, falling
short of expectation. Events will bear this out. The defective
circle mirrors the questionable reliability of the Rhinemaidens' forecast: 'The world's riches a man could inherit.' Such a
vague promise is the hallmark of all successful soothsayers.

Crisis

The ominous beats on the kettledrum will be heard at critical
moments, or when characters face a crucial or distressing
decision (see the Transition between Scenes 1 and 2 for a fuller
discussion).

Note on the Leitmotifs

The occurrence of each leitmotif is given beside the German text; at its first appearance, a motif is given in **bold** print. The syllable on which a leitmotif begins is shown by *italic* print (where no syllable is italicized, the motif begins after the line of text).

Where two motifs sound simultaneously, this is shown with a plus sign, e.g. 'Forge + Grief'; where motifs occur one after another, they are listed from left to right, e.g. 'Erda' (first motif), 'Grief' (following motif).

In naming the leitmotifs the author has adopted Hans von Wolzogen's nomenclature, where it was found to be helpful. For the sake of clarity, however, he has substituted his own terminology wherever necessary.

Running Commentary

Newcomers may wish to skip the commentary on the right of the translation at the first reading. Their value to the reader will, I hope, progressively increase.

1. Szene

Vorspiel

WOGLINDE

Innocence   *Wei*a! Waga!
Woge, du Welle!
Walle zur Wiege!
Wagalaweia!
Wallala weiala weia!

WELLGUNDE
Woglinde, wachst du allein?

WOGLINDE
Mit Wellgunde wär ich zu zwei.

WELLGUNDE
Lass sehn, wie du wachst.

WOGLINDE

Genesis   Sicher vor *dir*.

FLOSSHILDE
Heiala weia!
Wildes Geschwister!

WELLGUNDE
Flosshilde, schwimm!
Woglinde flieht:
hilf mir die Fliehende fangen!

FLOSSHILDE

Des Goldes Schlaf

Scene 1

Prelude

[At the bottom of the Rhine. Greenish twilight, swirling waters and humid mist. Jagged rocks everywhere. As the curtain rises, one of the Rhinemaidens circles the central rock.]

WOGLINDE
Weia! Waga!
Wandering waters,
cradle us, rock us.
Wagalaweia!
Wallala weiala weia!

Woglinde babbles, like the water.

The Innocence motif will later appear, rhythmically transformed, in Brünnhilde's slumber music (*Die Walküre*), and in the Woodbird's warbling (*Siegfried*).

WELLGUNDE [from above]
Woglinde, watching alone?

WOGLINDE
With Wellgunde we would be two.

WELLGUNDE [dives down to the rock]
How good is your guard? [she tries to catch Woglinde]

WOGLINDE
Catch if you can! [they chase and tease each other]

A game of aquatic tag.

The rhythm to which Wellgunde sings foreshadows the later Ride of the Valkyries (*Die Walküre*). Rhinemaidens and Valkyries represent the elements. Here, at the beginning of the world, the notes G–E flat–G–B flat form an open major chord. In the Ride of the Valkyries this changes to G–E flat (D sharp)–G–B natural, an ominous augmented chord: the world has lost its innocence and is halfway to perdition.

FLOSSHILDE [from above]
Heiala weia!
Frivolous sisters!

WELLGUNDE
Flosshilde, swim!
Woglinde flees.
Help me to capture the sleek one!

FLOSSHILDE [dives down to join her sisters]
The slumbering gold

Genesis hütet ihr schlecht;
besser bewacht
des Schlummernden Bett,
sonst büsst ihr beide das Spiel!

ALBERICH
He he! Ihr Nicker!
Wie seid ihr niedlich,
neidliches Volk!
Aus Nibelheims Nacht
naht ich mich gern,
neigtet ihr euch zu mir.

WOGLINDE
Hei! wer ist dort?

FLOSSHILDE
Es dämmert und ruft.

WELLGUNDE
Lugt, wer uns belauscht!

WOGLINDE und WELLGUNDE
Pfui! der Garstige!

FLOSSHILDE
Hütet das Gold!
Vater warnte
vor solchem Feind.

ALBERICH
Ihr, da oben!

DIE DREI
Was willst du dort unten?

ALBERICH
Stör ich eu'r Spiel,
wenn staunend ich still hier steh?
Tauchtet ihr nieder,
mit euch tollte
und neckte der Niblung sich gern!

slips from your guard.
Better protect
the sleeper's repose,
else you will pay for your pranks!
[She tries to catch them, but they elude her.
Alberich appears from the darkness below
and clambers upwards.]

ALBERICH
Hehe! you nixies!
Frolicsome fish,
desirable folk!
From Nibelheim's night
would I draw near.
Will you grant me your grace?
[at the sound of his voice, the maidens stop
frolicking]

WOGLINDE
Hei, who is there?

FLOSSHILDE
A voice from the gloom!

WELLGUNDE
See who seeks us out! [they dive down
and detect the Nibelung]

WOGLINDE and **WELLGUNDE**
Ugh! how horrible!

FLOSSHILDE [swiftly darting upwards]
Look to the gold!
Father warned us
of such a fiend. [all three gather round
the central rock]

ALBERICH
You above there!

ALL THREE
What is it, below there?

ALBERICH
Would you object,
if I just stood still and watched?
Do but dive deeper!
With you, romping
and rollicking would be fine fun!

Just before Alberich's first words
the violas illustrate his attempts
to climb the rock with a repeated,
jarring two-note figure. We are in
the presence of a potential
marauder.

Not Father Rhine, but a presumably primeval force that had
ordained the Rhinemaidens as
guardians of the gold, the security
of which ensures the security of
the world.

Alberich's instinct urges him
upwards: the longing of the ugly
for the beautiful.

'Alberich' is a title rather than a
name. Loge calls him 'Schwarz-
Alberich' (Lord of Darkness),
while in *Siegfried* Wotan will
name himself 'Licht-Alberich'
(Lord of Light).

At the beginning of *Das Rheingold* Alberich invades the Rhine.
At the end of *Götterdämmerung*
the Rhine is invaded by his son,
Hagen.

Lilli Lehmann, the first Woglinde
(1876) related: 'Strapped in tight
corsets, we were put into swimming machines. Each comprised
one cart and three manipulators.
One was the driver, another
worked the lift which moved us
up and down, and the third acted
as director of music, giving his
singer the necessary cues.'

WOGLINDE
Mit uns will er spielen?

WELLGUNDE
Ist ihm das Spott?

ALBERICH
Wie scheint im Schimmer
ihr hell und schön!
Wie gern umschlänge
der Schlanken eine mein Arm,
schlüpfte hold sie herab!

FLOSSHILDE
Nun lach ich der Furcht:
der Feind ist verliebt.

WELLGUNDE
Der lüsterne Kauz!

WOGLINDE
Lasst ihn uns kennen!

ALBERICH
Die neigt sich herab.

WOGLINDE
Alberich Nun nahe dich mir!

ALBERICH

Garstig glatter
glitschriger Glimmer!
Alberich Wie gleit ich aus!
Mit Händen und Füssen
nicht fasse noch halt ich
das schlecke Geschlüpfer!
Feuchtes Nass
füllt mir die Nase:
verfluchtes Niesen!

WOGLINDE
Prustend naht
meines Freiers Pracht.

WOGLINDE
He itches to join us.

WELLGUNDE
Is this a jest?

ALBERICH
You glow and glisten,
you matchless maids!
O let me pamper
and pet you, fondlesome folk!
Do but kindly come down!

Wagner told his wife, Cosima, that
he had a fellow-feeling for
Alberich.

FLOSSHILDE
I laugh at my fear:
our fiend is in love!

So long as he chases us,
Flosshilde reckons, he will not
chase the gold.

WELLGUNDE
The lecherous lout!

WOGLINDE
Teach him a lesson! [she approaches
the top of Alberich's rock]

A trap for translators: 'Lasst ihn
uns kennen' does not mean 'let
us get to know him' but 'let him
get to know us'. In other words,
'we love to tease, so let us tease
him.'

ALBERICH
She sinks down to me!

WOGLINDE
Come close, I am here.

The descending chromatic cello
figure that frames Alberich's
words denotes his discomfiture.

ALBERICH [tries to clamber to the top, but
keeps falling back]
Slippery, slimy,
ghastly glimmer!
I slip and slide;
my hands cannot hold
and my feet cannot fetter
those slithery nixies!
Nasty damp
tickles my nostrils:
accursed sneezing! [he has got close
to Woglinde]

Alberich is out of his depth, and
the temperature does not suit
him. Wagner illustrates this with
ten amusingly-intensified nasal
eruptions, produced by several
horns.

WOGLINDE [laughing]
Splutter on,
you my lovesick swain!

ALBERICH
Mein Friedel sei,
du fräuliches Kind!

WOGLINDE
Willst du mich frein,
so freie mich hier!

ALBERICH
O weh; du entweichst?
Komm doch wieder!
Schwer ward mir,
was so leicht du erschwingst.

WOGLINDE
Steig nur zu Grund:
da greifst du mich sicher!

ALBERICH
Wohl besser da unten!

WOGLINDE
Nun aber nach oben!

WELLGUNDE und FLOSSHILDE
Ha ha ha ha ha ha!

ALBERICH
Wie fang ich im Sprung
den spröden Fisch?
Warte, du Falsche!

WELLGUNDE
Heia! Du Holder!
Hörst du mich nicht?

ALBERICH
Rufst du nach mir?

WELLGUNDE
Ich rate dir wohl:
zu mir wende dich,
Woglinde meide!

ALBERICH
Viel schöner bist du

ALBERICH
Be mine, be mine,
voluptuous maid! [he attempts to
embrace her]

WOGLINDE [slipping away]
If you would court me,
court me up here! [she lands on
another rock]

ALBERICH [scratching his head]
Alas, do but stay!
Come down closer!
Hard for me
what is easy for you.

WOGLINDE [swims to another rock]
Brisk to the bottom,
for there you can hold me!

ALBERICH [clambers down]
Yes, yes, to the bottom!

WOGLINDE [darts upwards]
Now swift to the surface!

Rising violin semiquavers accompany Woglinde's escape. They ascend, however, by only one octave, suggesting that though she is out of his immediate reach she is still tantalizingly close.

WELLGUNDE and FLOSSHILDE
Ha ha ha ha ha ha!

ALBERICH
But how can I catch
this frigid fish?
Wait for me, false one! [he scrambles
after her]

Syncopated violins and violas mock Alberich's vain acrobatics.

WELLGUNDE [from a lower rock]
Greetings, fine fellow!
Listen to me!

ALBERICH [turning towards her]
Do you mean me?

WELLGUNDE
Be counselled by me:
attend Wellgunde!
Woglinde tricks you.

In his first prose sketch to *Das Rheingold* (1851) Wagner introduced Wotan 'bathing', presumably sharing the amenities of the river with Alberich and the Rhinemaidens.

ALBERICH [clambers hastily towards her]
I praise this sight.

als jene Scheue,
die minder gleissend
und gar zu glatt.
Nur tiefer tauche,
willst du mir taugen!

WELLGUNDE
Bin nun ich dir nah?

ALBERICH
Noch nicht genug!
Die schlanken Arme
schlinge um mich,
dass ich den Nacken
dir neckend betaste,
mit schmeichelnder Brunst
an die schwellende Brust mich dir
  schmiege.

WELLGUNDE
Bist du verliebt
und lüstern nach Minne,
lass sehn, du Schöner,
wie bist du zu schaun?
Pfui, du haariger,
höckriger Geck!
Schwarzes, schwieliges
Schwefelgezwerg!
Such dir ein Friedel,
dem du gefällst!

ALBERICH
Gefall ich dir nicht,
dich fass ich doch fest!

WELLGUNDE
Genesis   Nur fest, sonst fliess ich dir *fort*!

WOGLINDE und FLOSSHILDE
Ha ha ha ha ha ha!

ALBERICH
Kalter, grätiger Fisch!
Alberich   *Schein* ich nicht schön dir,
niedlich und neckisch,
glatt und glau –
hei! so buhle mit Aalen,
ist dir eklig mein Balg!

Your sister is prudish,
her face more sombre,
the slippery one.
Now dive down deeper,
be my own darling!

WELLGUNDE [coming a little closer]
How close shall I come?

ALBERICH
Close as you can!   A six-note chromatic cello figure,
Your arms so comely,   droned out sixteen times, accom-
coil round me now,   panies Alberich's salacious
that I may fondle   serenade.
your face with my fingers.
Enraptured, enthralled,
let me nuzzle your billowy bosom!

WELLGUNDE   Wellgunde inspects her suitor at
Are you in love,   close range. As she recoils, violas
my lecherous wooer?   pronounce their verdict on
Come then, and show me   Alberich's shortcomings. They imi-
how shapely you are.   tate Wellgunde's 'wie bist du zu
Ugh! you hideous,   schaun?' on their lowest strings,
twisted old troll!   while a muted horn adds a sneer
Sooty, scaly,   to their last note.
sulphurous runt!
Fish for a sweetheart   The Rhinemaidens are playing
foul as yourself!   with fire, advertising without any
                                                     intention of selling.
                          Wellgunde streaks to the top,
ALBERICH [clinging to her]   abetted by flute and clarinet, who
My face may be foul,   swoop upwards together with the
but firm is my grip.   immaculate savage.

WELLGUNDE [darting away]
So firm, I slip through your hands!

                                                     Their jeering laughter has an
WOGLINDE and FLOSSHILDE   ominous ring: genuine laughter
Ha ha ha ha ha ha!   rises, but theirs falls a semitone.
                                                     No good will come from such
ALBERICH   merriment.
Faithless thing!
So I'm not dainty,
pretty and playful,
sleek and smooth.
Take an eel for a lover,
if you find me so foul!

FLOSSHILDE

Was zankst du, Alb? Schon so
  verzagt?
Du freitest um zwei.
Frügst du die Dritte,
süssen Trost
schüfe die Traute dir!

ALBERICH

Holder Sang
singt zu mir her.
Wie gut, dass ihr
eine nicht seid!
Von vielen gefall ich wohl einer:
bei einer kieste mich keine!
Soll ich dir glauben,
so gleite herab!

FLOSSHILDE

Wie törig ihr seid,
dumme Schwestern,
dünkt euch dieser nicht schön?

ALBERICH

Für dumm und hässlich
darf ich sie halten,
Liebe-Tragik   seit ich dich *Hold*este seh.

FLOSSHILDE

O singe fort
so süss und fein:
wie hehr verführt es mein Ohr!

ALBERICH

Mir zagt, zuckt
und zehrt sich das Herz,
Liebe-Tragik   lacht mir so *zierl*iches Lob.

FLOSSHILDE

Wie deine Anmut
mein Aug erfreut,
deines Lächelns Milde
den Mut mir labt.
Seligster Mann!

ALBERICH

Süsseste Maid!

FLOSSHILDE
Stop sulking, dwarf, be not
    dismayed!
You only tried two,
now try the third one.
Her soft heart
promises rich reward.

ALBERICH
Sweetest song
soothes my ears.
What luck to meet
more than just one.
I might win me one out of many;
with one – I might not find any.
Shall I believe you,
so float to my arms!

FLOSSHILDE [dives down to him]
How feeble are you,
foolish sisters!
Noble is he and neat!

ALBERICH
Quite dull and graceless,
such are your sisters.
You are the fairest by far!

FLOSSHILDE
Sing on, sing on,
and weave your spells:
your song seduces my ears.

ALBERICH [touching her]
I shake, shift
and shudder with lust,
hearing such honey-sweet words.

FLOSSHILDE [gently restraining him]
O how your beauty
enchants my eyes;
how your smile so tender
entrances me! [she draws him to her]
Dearest of men!

ALBERICH
Daintiest maid!

The depth is lit up by a sudden
harp chord of A flat major, with
the 'blue' note G flat thrown in as
an erotic bonus. Alberich stands
enchanted. Where there is such
beauty, there must surely be
goodness also. He is ready to
wager his wounded heart for a
third time.

Alberich has been teased and
abused by Woglinde and Wellgunde, but his self-esteem has
not been destroyed. He dismisses
the present disaster with grim
humour: two gone, one to come.

So overcome is Alberich with the
possibilities of the situation that
he turns songster, matching the
lyricism of Flosshilde's serenade.
He even rises to a rhyming
couplet, though his confusion is
reflected in his confused arith-
metic.

Flosshilde treats Alberich to a
feast of descending major
seconds, hinting at the later Joy
motif.

FLOSSHILDE
Wärst du mir hold!

ALBERICH
Hielt' ich dich immer!

FLOSSHILDE
Deinen stechenden Blick,
deinen struppigen Bart,
o säh' ich ihn, fasst' ich ihn stets!
Deines stachligen Haares
strammes Gelock,
umflöss' es Flosshilde ewig!
Deine Krötengestalt,
deiner Stimme Gekrächz,
o dürft' ich staunend und stumm
sie nur hören und sehn!

WOGLINDE und **WELLGUNDE**
Ha ha ha ha ha ha!

ALBERICH
Lacht ihr Bösen mich aus?

FLOSSHILDE
Wie billig am Ende vom Lied.

WOGLINDE und **WELLGUNDE**
Ha ha ha ha ha ha!

ALBERICH
Grief   *We*he, ach wehe!
O Schmerz! O Schmerz!
Liebesnot   Die *dri*tte, so traut,
betrog sie mich auch?
Ihr schmählich schlaues,
lüderlich schlechtes Gelichter!
Nährt ihr nur Trug,
Innocence   ihr treuloses Nickergezücht?

DIE DREI
Wallala, wallala,
lalaleia, leialalei,
heia, heia, ha ha!
Schäme dich, Albe!
Schilt nicht dort unten!
Höre, was wir dich heissen!
Warum, du Banger,
bandest du nicht

FLOSSHILDE
Were you but mine!

ALBERICH
Yours and for ever!

FLOSSHILDE [clasping him]
To be pierced by your stare,
to be pricked by your stubble,
ever to live in your love!
Let your porcupine plumage,
fuzzy and foul,
but float round Flosshilde's bosom!
How you twitch like a toad,
as you creak, as you croak:
amazed, admiring and mute
let me hear and behold!

WOGLINDE and **WELLGUNDE**
Ha ha ha ha ha ha!

ALBERICH [alarmed]
Are you trifling with me?

FLOSSHILDE [darting away]
So ends our gallant affair!

WOGLINDE and **WELLGUNDE**
Ha ha ha ha ha ha!

ALBERICH [screeching]
Torment and torture!
Alas, alas!
The third, the dear third,
she too is a cheat.
You shifty, shameless,
slovenly, slippery strumpets!
Tricksters and snakes!
You watery witches! You trulls!

ALL THREE
Wallala, wallala,
lalaleia, leialalei,
heia, heia, ha ha!
Shame on you, goblin,
chide us no longer!
Stay, and hear what we tell you.
You are too timid!
Take and hold tight

This is the exalted language of *Tristan und Isolde*, and the chromatic music foreshadows the second act of that drama.

She holds him close in her arms, a position conducive to illusion and disillusion alike.

Flosshilde has forgotten her earlier injunction, 'Father warned us of such a fiend.' Father might also have cautioned against rousing a man's appetite without providing the means for stilling it. Especially not a fiend's.

Alberich's tormented cries on the falling semitone establish the symbol for grief, one of the most frequently occurring motifs in the *Ring*.

The submarine world is asplash with jubilation. The Rhinemaidens carol, babble and gurgle. Violins and violas flood the orchestra with their Genesis semiquavers, while the woodwind intone the Innocence motif. But Alberich – who has sacrificed his sanity, such as it was, on the slippery altar of desire – is about to destroy the existing world order.

das Mädchen, das du minnst?
Treu sind wir
und ohne Trug
dem Freier, der uns fängt.
Greife nur zu
und grause dich nicht!

Innocence   In der *Flut* entfliehn wir nicht
   leicht.
Wallala, lalaleia,
leialalei,
heia, heia, hahei!

ALBERICH
Wie in den Gliedern
brünstige Glut
mir brennt und glüht!
Wut und Minne
wild und mächtig
wühlt mir den Mut auf!
Wie ihr auch lacht und lügt,
lüstern lechz ich nach euch,

Alberich   *Innocence*   und eine muss mir erliegen!
Alberich   *Innocence*
   Alberich

ALBERICH
Fing' eine diese Faust!

Rhinegold

WOGLINDE
Lugt, Schwestern!
Rhinegold   Die Weckerin lacht in den Grund.

WELLGUNDE
Durch den grünen Schwall
den wonnigen Schläfer sie grüsst.

FLOSSHILDE
Jetzt küsst sie sein Auge,
dass er es öffne.

WELLGUNDE
Rhinegold   *Schaut*, er lächelt
in lichtem Schein.

the darling you desire!
True are we,
true without tricks,
to him who holds us fast.
Tackle us then,
fish and fall to!
It is hard to flee in the
    flood.
Wallala, lalaleia,
leialalei,
heia, heia, hahei! [they swim apart,
inviting Alberich to chase them]

ALBERICH
Fiercely within me
rages a fire;
my soul's aflame!
Lust and longing,
mad and frantic,
torture my manhood.
Well may you laugh and lie,
yet I yearn for your love,
and one of you must content me!
[He pursues them over the rocks, staggers,
clambers up again, almost but not quite
catching them. They tease him mercilessly.
At last he shakes his fist, foaming with rage.]

Strings mock Alberich's desperate
attempts to clamber up the rock
and echo his feverish marine
mountaineering music, their frantic semiquavers splashing all over
the passionate dwarf. The woodwind play the Innocence motif:
the Rhinemaidens are free from
care, and careless.

ALBERICH
This fist shall teach you fear!
[A bright glow penetrates the waters from
above. Alberich is spellbound.]

He shakes his fist at the world.
Woodwind and horns snarl a dot-
ted rhythm which in Scene 3 will
be associated with the forging of
golden wealth. This is the
moment when Alberich, the
rejected suitor, emerges as a can-
didate for loveless dominion of
the universe.

WOGLINDE
Look, sisters!
The sunlight bedazzles the deep.

WELLGUNDE
In the emerald waves
she smiles and awakens the gold.

First and second violins play a
triplet figure which is first given
by twelve players in three parts,
then sixteen players in four parts,
twenty-four players in six parts,
and finally by thirty-two players in
eight parts. The effect matches
the stage event: dazzling light
illuminating the water.

FLOSSHILDE
She kisses its eyelid,
so it will open.

WELLGUNDE
See it smile now,
our radiant star!

WOGLINDE
Durch die Fluten hin

Rhinegold   fliesst sein strahlender Stern.

DIE DREI
Heiajaheia, heiajaheia,
wallala lalala leiajahei!

Joy   *Rhein*gold, Rheingold!
Leuchtende Lust,
wie lachst du so hell und
    hehr!
Glühender Glanz
entgleisst dir weihlich im Wag!
Heiajaheia, heiajaheia!
Wache, Freund,
wache froh!
Wonnige Spiele
spenden wir dir:
flimmert der Fluss,
flammet die Flut,
umfliessen wir tauchend,
tanzend und singend
im seligen Bade dein Bett.

Joy   *Rhein*gold, Rheingold!
Heiajaheia, heiajaheia,

Rhinegold   wallala lalala leiaja*hei*!

ALBERICH

Was ist's, ihr Glatten,
das dort so glänzt und gleisst?

DIE DREI
Wo bist du Rauher denn heim,
dass vom Rheingold nicht du
    gehört?

WELLGUNDE
Nicht weiss der Alb
von des Goldes Auge,
das wechselnd wacht und schläft?

WOGLINDE
Von der Wassertiefe
wonnigem Stern,
der hehr die Wogen durchhellt?

WOGLINDE
Through the flowing tide
breaks a brilliant light!

ALL THREE [swimming around the rock]
Heiajaheia, heiajaheia,
wallala lalala leiajahei!
Rhinegold, Rhinegold,
jubilant joy!
How brave and how bright your
  smile.
Noble the glow,
and glorious the glittering gold!
Heiajaheia, heiajaheia!
Waken, friend!
Wake to joy!
Marvellous games
we'll play in your praise!
Waters aflame,
fiery flood:
as floating around you,
dancing and singing,
we dive and we bathe in your bed.
Rhinegold, Rhinegold,
heiajaheia, heiajaheia,
wallala lalala leiajahei! [They circle
the rock in exuberant joy. The river glitters
with golden radiance.]

ALBERICH [attracted by the gleam, he
stares at the gold]
What is it, sleek ones?
What glows and gleams up there?

ALL THREE
Where are you, ruffian, at home?
Of the Rhinegold have you not
  heard?

WELLGUNDE
He does not know
of the eye of gold,
which would wake and sleep in
  turn.

WOGLINDE
In the rushing waves,
our radiant star
so lordly lightens the deep.

Their jubilation is triggered by
successive cymbal and triangle
beats. The key is C major, and
since Wagner has so far withheld
this tonality of light and joy its
impact now is as stunning as
Haydn's 'And it was light!' at the
beginning of *The Creation*.

The twenty-two-bar section,
beginning with the Joy motif and
ending with 'Heiajaheia!', is a
hosanna to happiness, with
strings, woodwind, horns, timpani, harps, triangle and cymbals
rejoicing in fellow abandon.

The 1869 Munich performance
was clumsily staged. One critic,
unimpressed with the Rhinemaidens' gyrations, called the scene 'a
whore-house aquarium'. For his
pains, he was taken to court by
the husband of Frau Vogl (Wellgunde), who felt that his wife's
honour had been besmirched.

Now the slope from exuberance
to fatal negligence is slippery
indeed.

Nature myths from all over the
world draw parallels between
gold underground and the sun in
the sky. In Indian mythology,
dwarfs captured the gold of the
sun, and kept it hidden inside a
mountain. In the 'kennings' of
Norse poetry gold is known as
'ship of the dwarfs', 'star of the
depth', 'flame of the waters' or
'Rhine fire'. But the location of the
Rhinegold and its theft by
Alberich are Wagner's own inven-
tion, as is the philosophical
implication of misusing a thing of
beauty for mercenary ends.

DIE DREI
Sieh, wie selig
im Glanze wir gleiten!
Willst du Banger
in ihm dich baden,

Innocence   so *schwimm* und schwelge mit uns!
Rhinegold   Wall*ala* lala leialalei,
wallala lala leiajahei!

ALBERICH
Eurem Taucherspiele
nur taugte das Gold?
Mir gält' es dann wenig!

WOGLINDE
Des Goldes Schmuck
schmähte er nicht,
wüsste er all seine Wunder!

WELLGUNDE

Ring   Der *Welt* Erbe
gewänne zu eigen,
wer aus dem Rheingold
schüfe den Ring,
der masslose Macht ihm verlieh'.

FLOSSHILDE
Der Vater sagt' es,
und uns befahl er,
klug zu hüten
den klaren Hort,
dass kein Falscher der Flut
   ihn entführe:
drum schweigt, ihr schwatzendes
   Heer!

WELLGUNDE
Du klügste Schwester,
verklagst du uns wohl?
Weisst du denn nicht,
wem nur allein
das Gold zu schmieden vergönnt?

WOGLINDE

Liebe-Tragik   Nur wer der *Min*ne
Macht versagt,
nur wer der Liebe
Lust verjagt,

ALL THREE
See how blithely
we glide in its glory!
Be not fearful,
and join our frolics!
Come, splash in splendour with us!
Wallala lala leialalei,
wallala lala leiajahei!

The three are delirious and past
caring, or they would not dare to
invite Alberich to join their revels.

ALBERICH
For your gambols only
the gold should be good?
What use is such plunder?

WOGLINDE
Our golden toy
he would adore
could he discover its secret.

WELLGUNDE
The world's riches
a man could inherit,
who from the Rhinegold
fashioned the ring
that made him the lord of the
    world.

Woodwind intone the Ring motif
which, throughout the tetralogy,
will be heard when the fatal ring
is contemplated, won or lost. Its
musical shape resembles an
incomplete circle and hints at the
flaws in the ring itself.

FLOSSHILDE
Our father told us,
and made us guardians,
faithful guardians
of all the gold,
lest some rogue should defraud the
    deep waters.
On guard then, gossiping girls!

There is much chromatic anxiety
in Flosshilde's warning.

WELLGUNDE
Our prudent sister,
reprove us no more.
Surely you know,
one man alone
can forge the ring from the gold.

WOGLINDE
He who can close
his heart to love,
he who denies
the law of love.

The listener is alerted to the
weightiness of Woglinde's
proclamation: it is reinforced by a
contrabass trombone, two tenor
tubas, two bass tubas, a contrabass tuba, strings and timpani.

nur der erzielt sich den Zauber,

Ring   zum *Reif* zu zwingen das Gold.

WELLGUNDE
Wohl sicher sind wir und
    sorgenfrei,

Liebe-Tragik   denn was nur *lebt*, will lieben;
meiden will keiner die Minne.

WOGLINDE
Am wenigsten er,
der lüsterne Alb:
vor Liebesgier
möcht er vergehn!

FLOSSHILDE
Nicht fürcht ich den,
wie ich ihn erfand:
seiner Minne Brunst
brannte fast mich.

WELLGUNDE

Ring   Ein *Schwe*felbrand
in der Wogen Schwall:
vor Zorn der Liebe

Innocence   zischt er laut.

DIE DREI
Wallala wallaleia lala!
Lieblichster Albe,
lachst du nicht auch?
In des Goldes Scheine
wie leuchtest du schön!
O komm, Lieblicher,
lache mit uns!
Heiajaheia, heiajaheia,

Rhinegold   wallala lala*la* leiajahei!

Joy   *Ring*

ALBERICH

Ring   Der *Welt* Erbe
gewänn' ich zu eigen durch dich?

Ring   *Erz*wäng' ich nicht Liebe,

Liebe-Tragik   doch listig erzwäng' mir *Lust*?
Spottet nur zu!
Der Niblung naht eurem Spiel!

that man may summon the magic
to wrest a ring from the gold.

WELLGUNDE
We need not fret and we need not
    fear:
man lives by love forever.
None could last out without loving.

WOGLINDE
And least of all he,
the lecherous dwarf.
His drooling lust
wastes him away.

FLOSSHILDE
I fear him not,
I fathomed his heart.
In his passion's flames
Flosshilde burned!

WELLGUNDE
A brimstone-brand
in the surging waves!
Such furious frenzy,
hissing loud!

ALL THREE
Wallala wallaleia lala!
Lovable elf-man,
laugh with us now!
In the golden glory
you too appear fair.
So come, radiant one,
revel with us!
Heiajaheia, heiajaheia,
wallala lalala leiajahei! [they laugh
and swim in the glow]

ALBERICH [his eyes fixed on the gold]
The world's riches
were mine if I ravished the gold?
Where love is forbidden,
I still could enforce its delights?
Mock as you will,
the Niblung makes for your toy!
[Furiously, he clambers to the top of
the rock. The maidens cry out and swim
apart.]

With so much hypnotic reiteration of the Ring motif in his ears, Alberich's mind is made up for him. He pays no attention to the E major adoration of golden beauty for golden beauty's sake, which the Rhinemaidens invite him to share, but is seduced by the rhythm of their exultant 'Heia-jaheia!' (a rhythm which will assume a fearful aspect in Scene 3, when Alberich's Nibelung slaves will mine and hammer the gold to its murderous monotony).

Since love is not available for the likes of Alberich, he will purchase its delights. On his word 'Lust', strings and horn sound the Liebe-Tragik motif. The tragedy of love is about to manifest itself. Love enslaved, love denied, love despised and love betrayed will all grow in intensity as we progress through the *Ring*. It will take another work altogether, *Parsifal*, for love to be the redeeming catalyst.

DIE DREI

Heia heia heiajahei!
Rettet euch!
Es raset der Alb!
In den Wassern sprüht's,
wohin er springt.
Die Minne macht ihn verrückt!
Hahaha haha haha!

ALBERICH

Bangt euch noch nicht?
So buhlt nun im Finstern,
feuchtes Gezücht!
Das Licht *lösch* ich euch aus;
entreisse dem *Riff* das Gold,
schmiede den rächenden *Ring*;
denn hör es die Flut:
so verfluch ich die Liebe!

FLOSSHILDE

Haltet den Räuber!

WELLGUNDE

Rettet das Gold!

WOGLINDE und WELLGUNDE

Hilfe! Hilfe!

DIE DREI

Weh! Weh!

Alberich

Rhinegold
Rhinegold
Rhinegold
Ring

Liebe-Tragik

Rhinegold

ALL THREE
Heia heia heiajahei!
Save yourselves,
the man has gone mad!
See the waters spurt,
where he has sprung.
Desire has cost him his wits.
Hahaha haha haha!

ALBERICH
Still not dismayed?
Make love in the dark then,
fishified fools! [he reaches for the gold]
Your light, let it go out!
I plunder your precious gold,
forge the avenging ring!
Bear witness, the world:
curst be love and all loving! [He tears
the gold from the rock, swoops down with
it and disappears. All at once, darkness
descends. The Rhinemaidens plunge down
in vain pursuit.]

FLOSSHILDE
Round on the robber!

WELLGUNDE
Rescue the gold!

WOGLINDE and WELLGUNDE
Help us! Help us!

ALL THREE
Woe! Woe! [Alberich's triumphant laughter can be heard from below. The waters
recede, the rocks disappear. Black billows
change to lighter mist and clouds.]

Alberich pronounces his curse to
the Liebe-Tragik motif which,
instead of its usual stepwise
descent, suddenly plunges down
by a seventh on the second syllable of 'Liebe'. Alberich's view of
love is now distorted, the composer seems to suggest.

The Rhinemaidens disappear,
submerged by the falling waters,
by the falling cello semiquavers
and by Alberich's mocking
laughter.
     This is not their final exit from
the *Ring*. Their unseen presence
will haunt the end of *Das Rheingold*, when their demand for the
return of the gold clouds the
gods' joyful entry into Walhall; at
the end of the Prologue to *Götterdämmerung* their music reminds
Siegfried that the ring was not his
to dispose of, and that fatal consequences are at hand.

The curse of Alberich even haunt-
ed the first performance of *Die
Walküre* at Bayreuth in 1876. Herr
Vogl, whose pregnant wife had to
withdraw from the cast, apolo-
gised to Wagner in writing: 'My
wife is to become a mother, but is
horrified at having to forgo the
good fortune of singing at
Bayreuth. Please forgive me, for I
was quite unable to emulate
Alberich's curse on love.'

We shall meet them once more,
at the end of the drama. By then
the Rhinemaidens, while retaining
their tendency for frivolity and
breeziness, will have gained much
worldly wisdom. They will claim
the mandate of justice which the
gods had long relinquished. They
will grant to Hagen, son of
Alberich, what they had denied
the father, close bodily contact
and deadly embrace. Once again
they will assume guardianship of
the gold.

Transition

Alberich has made off with the gold. Love is no longer his
ambition. He is guided by Wellgunde's promise, 'The world's
riches a man could inherit, who from the Rhinegold fashioned
the ring that made him the lord of the world.' How reliable is
Wellgunde's forecast? In Scene 3 Alberich, though lord of the
ring, is nonetheless tricked and captured. In Scene 4 he surrenders it to Wotan, not before cursing it and its future owners. As it turns out, Alberich's curse will prove far more potent
than Wellgunde's prediction. Fafner kills his brother over the
ring, only to lose it and his life to Siegfried (*Siegfried*, Act II). At
the beginning of *Götterdämmerung* Siegfried gives the ring to
Brünnhilde, as a love token. It does not help her, however,
when Siegfried, in disguise, robs her of it (Act I). In Acts II and
III, moreover, the ring will become crucial evidence which
leads to Siegfried's execution. At the end of the tetralogy
Brünnhilde will take the ring from the dead Siegfried's hand
and return it, at last, to the Rhinemaidens. Hagen, son of
Alberich, is to drown in its pursuit, and Alberich's curse will
drown with it. So does the illusion of its measureless might.

Alberich puts his faith in the golden booty. It is in accord
with ancient lore that he should gain power by renouncing
love, for in Teutonic tradition the finder and possessor of
treasure must be pure in mind and not encumbered by love.
Alberich fulfils the second requirement, at any rate. It is remark-
able that Wagner's first draft does not contain the curse on love
at all. Neither do the gods perish at the end. Brünnhilde restores
the ring to the river, and Wotan reigns supreme. But in his
revised prose sketch (1851), the author thinks aloud:

> The gold gleams. How can it be won? By him who will
> renounce love. Alberich ravishes the gold. Night.

Alberich's curse on the ring is not to take place until Scene 4.
What the dwarf now holds is the raw material which will
yield this supposed token of limitless power. The curse on
love, however, is operative from now on, and it would appear
that Alberich's spell has more than private significance, and
has become all-pervasive. Love is to become a marketable
commodity.

The Music: from the Depths of the Rhine to the Mountain Heights

The composer's task is to transport us, visually and aurally, from the Rhinemaidens' habitat to the domain of the gods. His stage directions are precise:

> Gradually, the waves change into clouds, and then into a fine mist which is illuminated from behind by an increasingly bright light of dawn. The mist disappears aloft, in the form of delicate little clouds, while in the early light an open space on a mountain height comes into view. On a flowery bank Wotan and Fricka, both asleep, are reposing side by side.

Alberich's demonic laughter concluded the first scene. The orchestra takes us now, in the space of fifty-one bars, from the depths to the heights. The upward motion is suggested, on stage, by a gradual change from darkness to light, from water to clouds, and from clouds to mist. The string instruments sweep in a long crescendo in C minor, gathering together all the forces of the orchestra. The tension subsides, and above sustained brass chords the Grief motif is heard twice, on oboe and cor anglais. Immediately, horn and cor anglais intone the Liebe-Tragik motif. The world grieves over the tragedy of bartered love. This seven-bar statement of the Liebe-Tragik motif is in effect a reiteration of Woglinde's earlier prediction,

> He who can close his heart to love, he who denies the law of love, that man may summon the magic to wrest a ring from the gold.

The motif is first accompanied by the timpani, *pianissimo*:

These drum beats announce one of the most important and least understood motifs in the whole *Ring*. They become more prominent, as they accompany the end of this section:

𝄞 ♩♩ | ♪ 𝄾 ♪♩♪ 𝄾 𝄾 𝄾 ♩♩ | ♪

Those ominous beats will be heard at critical moments. We shall encounter them in two forms:

or

The motif appears when Fasolt is clubbed to death by his brother (Scene 4). We hear it in *Walküre*, when Brünnhilde tells Siegmund of his impending death, and again when Siegmund is killed by Hunding. It adds its grim comment when Wotan is about to punish Brünnhilde. It is present when Wotan informs Mime (in *Siegfried*), that the dwarf will lose his head to the young hero. In *Götterdämmerung* it witnesses the slaying of Siegfried. We call it the motif of Crisis.

At the end of the transition the Liebe-Tragik motif gives way to the Ring motif, played by cor anglais and three clarinets. This particular combination of instruments was favoured by Wagner for this motif, possibly because of its veiled, dusky sound. The Ring motif is heard again, on woodwind and then on the violas, before being taken up, *pianissimo*, by two horns. But the transition is not yet complete. The composer reserves his master stroke for the very beginning of the next scene, when it will become clear that those last horn snatches of the Ring motif were, in fact, a pre-echo of the Walhall motif, Wotan's own noble motto.

Wagner revelled in his mastery of such orchestral transitions. He informed his beloved Mathilde Wesendonck: 'The subtlest and most profound aspect of my technique is the art of transition.' He compares his scenes to pillars, and continues: 'Now come and see how I have spanned those pillars.' Excited by the successful completion of Scene 1, Wagner wrote to Franz Liszt:

My friend, I am in the land of miracles! A new world lies before me. The great scene is finished. It contains unsuspected riches. I think I am at the height of my power. Every fibre of my being throbs with music.

Rhinemaidens as seen in the
Bayreuth production by Alfred
Kirchner, 1990s

Wotan and Fricka asleep in
front of Walhall; lithograph by
Franz Stassen (1914)

2
Scene

Synopsis
Leitmotifs
Libretto

Scene 2: Story

Open Space on a Mountain Top

Wotan hails his new fortress, Walhall, which the giants Fasolt
and Fafner have built for him. His wife Fricka reminds him of
the price he agreed to pay the giants – Freia, her own beautiful
young sister. Wotan plays for time, expecting shortly to hear
from Loge, his sly adviser, when Freia hastens to the scene,
pursued by the giants. Freia's brothers, Donner and Froh, are
unable to protect the goddess, while Wotan refuses to accede to
the giants' demands. Loge arrives at last. He reports Alberich's
theft of the Rhinegold and renunciation of love. He also dis-
closes that Alberich has succeeded in forging a ring from the
gold. The giants are now prepared to revoke their original
agreement, provided Wotan procures Alberich's gold for them.
Wotan, however, wishes to obtain the ring for himself. The
giants carry Freia off, and the gods begin to grow feeble and
old, since they are no longer sustained by Freia's golden
apples. Wotan resolves to descend to Nibelheim, Alberich's
abode. Guided by Loge, he plans to win Alberich's gold.

Freia's golden apples;
illustration by Arthur
Rackham (1909)

Scene 2: Action

1. Orchestra: Introduction
2. Fricka wakes the dreaming Wotan
3. Wotan greets Walhall
4. Wotan parries Fricka's reproaches
5. Freia demands help: Wotan relies on Loge
6. Giants demand their wages
7. Wotan refuses
8. Fasolt as moralist
9. Fasolt's grief
10. Golden Apples plot
11. Donner and Froh guard Freia
12. Wotan remonstrates with Donner
13. Loge's sophistry
14. Loge's narration
15. Loge's report causes confusion
16. Wotan and giants as contestants for the gold
17. Freia abducted
18. Gods grow old
19. Wotan resolves to obtain the ring
20. Orchestra: Wotan's and Loge's descent into Nibelheim

Fasolt and Fafner seize
Freia; lithograph by Franz
Stassen (1914)

Scene 2: Leitmotifs

The leitmotifs new to the scene follow in chronological order, together with the page number of first appearance.

Walhall   p.58

Treaty   p.58

Giants   p.58

Enchantment   p.60

Freia   p.62

Loge   p.66

Troth p.68

Golden Apples p.68

Forge p.80

Commentary on the Leitmotifs

Walhall

Derived from the Ring motif, the symbol of Alberich's power, the Walhall motif is the symbol of Wotan's power. Thirteen brass instruments (trumpets, trombones, bass trumpet, Wagner tubas*, contrabass tuba and contrabass trombone) announce it at the beginning of the second scene. This is the only time when the majestic motif is played in its entirety of twenty bars.

*Wagner's specially designed tenor and bass tubas, whose narrow bore and funnel-shaped mouthpiece achieve a tone which blends perfectly with the horns.

Treaty

This step-wise descending motif finds its visual equivalent in Wotan's lowered spear (the symbol of the god's laws and treaties). Wotan first obtained the spear by cutting a branch from the World Ash Tree, a feat which eventually caused the tree to wither.

Giants

Bass trumpet, trombones, contra bass tuba, strings and timpani give an accurate picture of the large-limbed, lumbering brothers, Fafner and Fasolt. The Giants motif pervades *Das Rheingold*, but thereafter is heard only once in *Die Walküre*, and just three times in *Siegfried*, then no more.

Enchantment

A rarely heard motif, which makes only eight appearances altogether, four times in *Das Rheingold* and four times in *Siegfried*. It is first sung by Fricka when she tries to curb Wotan's appetite for extra-mural activities, reminding him of the enchantment which awaits him in his own home: 'Handsome our palace, precious our household, such as to charm you to cherish our home.' The falling seventh represents Fricka's coy coquetry.

Freia

Violins play this motif, which accompanies Freia's flight from the giants. Its second half constitutes the Liebesnot motif which we have met in Scene 1. The Freia motif expresses inner turmoil, caused by or connected with erotic emotions. Freia is the goddess of beauty and of love, and her motif, at its first appearance, stands for love pursued.

Loge

Loge, like his flickering motif, personifies fire, man's servant or master. His chromatic music is in no key. Equivocal and elusive, it is played by string instruments. Its presence is felt most forcefully at the end of *Das Rheingold*, as it twines around Loge's pronouncement: 'They are rushing straight to their end, and they think they are gods everlasting. Ashamed I feel to sit at their table. My passion for fire, for flushes and flashes will no more be denied. To feast on those who had fettered my force, not to end blindly with those blind gods.'

Troth

Infrequently heard, this motif expresses the pledge between two parties, hence the canonic treatment (one voice entering after another). At its first appearance, Fafner's words 'Will you not fairly, honest and free be true to your barter and bond' form the first voice of the canon. The second is marked by cellos and double basses.

Golden Apples

'Golden apples grow in the goddess's garden,' announces Fafner, accompanied by the horns. Freia's golden apples endow the gods with eternal youth. The motif has a youthful ring, expressed by its unsophisticated melody and its vigorous rhythm.

Forge

Alberich's Nibelung slaves toil for their master to the murderous monotony of this battering rhythm. Ironically, the Rhinemaidens' joyous adoration of the gold, 'Heia jaheia!' (Scene 1), had the same rhythm. It is a brief step from joy to joylessness. Schubert anticipated the motif in the Scherzo of his Quartet in D minor:

2. Szene

FRICKA

Ring Wotan, Gemahl, erwache!

WOTAN

Ring Der Wonne seligen *Saal*
Walhall bewachen mir Tür und Tor:
Mannes Ehre,
ewige Macht,
ragen zu endlosem Ruhm!

FRICKA
Auf, aus der Träume
wonnigem Trug!
Walhall Erwache, Mann, und erwäge!

WOTAN
Vollendet das ewige Werk:
auf Berges Gipfel
die Götter-Burg,
prächtig strahlt
der prangende Bau!
Wie im Traum ich ihn trug,
wie mein Wille ihn wies,
stark und schön
steht er zur Schau;
hehrer, herrlicher Bau!

FRICKA
Nur Wonne schafft dir
was mich erschreckt?
Dich freut die Burg,
mir bangt es um Freia.
Achtloser, lass dich erinnern
Treaty des ausbedungenen Lohns!
Die Burg ist fertig,
verfallen das Pfand:
Giants vergassest du, was du ver*gabst*?

Scene 2

The previous scene can be regarded as a prelude. Scene 2 begins with the gods, in the key of D flat major. The gods are also at the end of the final drama, *Götterdämmerung*, and the key is again D flat major.

[Open space on a mountain top. Early morning. In the background rises a castle with bright battlements.]

FRICKA
Wotan, my lord, awaken!

WOTAN [still dreaming]
These halls of heavenly bliss
are guarded by gates and bolts.
Manhood's honour,
measureless might:
promise of peerless renown.

Wotan dreams, as the music tells us, not only of Walhall, but also of the ring.

FRICKA
Rise from those dreams
of easeful deceit.
Awaken, man, and consider!

WOTAN [wakes and beholds the castle]
Achieved is the hallowed abode.
On mountain summit
the gods' own gates.
Solid, proud,
the swaggering pile!
What my dream has desired,
what my will has designed,
bright and brave
stands it up there:
fortress radiant and rare.

FRICKA
The deed that thrills you
fills me with dread.
The fort is yours,
my fear is for Freia.
Reckless one, let me remind you
that contracts must be kept.
The work is finished,
the work must be paid.
Remember the bond that you
pledged!

At this point, the Giants motif is still incomplete. The kettledrum alone plays its ponderous rhythm.

WOTAN

Wohl dünkt mich's, was sie
   bedangen,

Treaty   die dort die Burg mir gebaut;
Durch Vertrag zähmt' ich
ihr trotzig Gezücht,
dass sie die hehre
Halle mir schüfen;
die steht nun, Dank den Starken:
um den Sold sorge dich nicht.

FRICKA

O lachend frevelnder Leichtsinn!
Liebelosester Frohmut!
Wusst' ich um euren Vertrag,
dem Truge hätt' ich gewehrt;
doch mutig entfernet
ihr Männer die Frauen,
um taub und ruhig vor uns
allein mit den Riesen zu tagen.
So ohne Scham
verschenktet ihr Frechen
Freia, mein holdes Geschwister,
froh des Schächergewerbs.
Was ist euch Harten
doch heilig und wert,
Ring   giert ihr Männer nach *Macht*!

WOTAN

Gleiche Gier

Ring   war Fricka wohl *fremd*,
als um den Bau sie mich bat?

FRICKA

Um des Gatten Treue besorgt
muss traurig ich wohl sinnen,
wie an mich er zu fesseln,
zieht's in die Ferne ihn fort:
Enchantment   *herr*liche Wohnung,
wonniger Hausrat,
sollten dich binden
zu säumender Rast.
Doch du bei dem Wohnbau sannst
auf Wehr und Wall allein:
Herrschaft und Macht
soll er dir mehren;
nur rastlosern Sturm zu erregen
Enchantment   erstand dir die ragende Burg.

WOTAN

I have not forgotten my
  bargain
with those who built me the fort;
for my terms tamed
that belligerent brood,
that they should raise
these glorious ramparts.
Both men have done their duty.
Pay no heed, wife, to the price.

FRICKA

What wanton, frivolous folly,
wilful, loveless and flippant!
Had I but known of your deal,
I would have checked your deceit.
When men drive brave bargains,
they banish their women,
that safe and separate from us
you might hobnob with the giants.
Had you no shame,
when bluntly you bartered
Freia, my beautiful sister,
sold to serve your conceit?
Cold is your heart,
and your heart does not care.
Men will lust after might.

WOTAN

Such a lust
did Fricka not feel,
when boldly she begged for the
  fort?

FRICKA

My concern for Wotan's good faith
would force me to consider
how to keep him beside me,
should he slip loose from his spouse.
Handsome our palace,
precious our household,
such as to charm you
to cherish our home.
But you, for our homestead, dreamt
of walls and war alone.
Lordship and power,
those are your passion.
To be but a cause for contention,
this castle was built for my lord.

Wotan personifies political man.
He is a pragmatist, his treaties are
based on expediency. While he
believes in power as a deterrent,
he persuades himself that his
actions are based on moral law.

In pawning Freia, the goddess of
love and beauty, Wotan is close to
renouncing love, like Alberich.

In having a fortress built for himself, Wotan exchanges the 'Freie
Gegend auf Bergeshöhen' (open
space on a mountain top) for
'hehrer, herrlicher Bau' (fortress
radiant and rare). From wilder-
ness to civilization, or from freedom to militancy?

WOTAN

Enchantment

Wolltest du Frau
in der Feste mich fangen,
mir Gotte musst du schon gönnen,
dass, in der Burg
gebunden, ich mir

Walhall

von *aus*sen gewinne die Welt.
Wandel und Wechsel
liebt wer lebt:
das Spiel drum kann ich nicht
  sparen.

FRICKA

Liebeloser,
leidiger Mann!
Um der Macht und Herrschaft
müssigen Tand
verspielst du in lästerndem Spott

Liebe-Tragik

Liebe und Weibes Wert?

Treaty

WOTAN

Um dich zum Weib zu gewinnen,
mein eines Auge
setzt ich werbend daran:
wie töricht tadelst du jetzt.
Ehr' ich die Frauen
doch mehr als dich freut.
Und Freia, die gute,
geb ich nicht auf:
nie sann dies ernstlich mein Sinn.

FRICKA

So schirme sie jetzt:
in schutzloser Angst

Freia

läuft sie nach Hilfe dort *her*!

Liebesnot

FREIA

Hilf mir, Schwester!
Schütze mich, Schwäher!
Vom Felsen drüben
drohte mir Fasolt,

Giants

mich Holde käm' er zu *hol*en.

WOTAN

Lass ihn drohn!
Sahst du nicht Loge?

FRICKA

Dass am liebsten du immer

WOTAN
If it befits
my own wife to confine me,
her lord must also be granted
that, if at home
imprisoned, he will
find freedom to conquer the world.
Ranging and changing,
life's own law –
that thrill I cannot relinquish.

FRICKA
Loveless consort,
cold-hearted man!
Is not power and rule
but tinsel and toy,
for Wotan to barter away
Freia, the light of love!

WOTAN
Recall the time when I wooed you:
one eye I yielded,
for to win you as wife.
Why will you rail at me now?
Women I cherish
far more than you like;
and Freia, our fair one,
is not for sale.
Such thoughts are far from my mind.

FRICKA
Then cherish her now!
In dread and distress,
see how she hastens for help.

FREIA [in hasty flight]
Save me, sister!
Wotan, protect me!
That mountain menace,
Fasolt, has threatened
to come and claim me as consort.

WOTAN
Let him claim!
Have you seen Loge?

FRICKA
Put your faith in that trickster

'If it befits my own wife to confine me ...' The music underlines Wotan's heavy irony: he quotes Fricka's Enchantment motif back at her.

The thirteenth-century Icelandic Edda, one of Wagner's sources for the *Ring*, tells of Wotan forfeiting one eye to drink from the fountain of wisdom. Wagner substitutes concrete for abstract, Fricka for wisdom.

dem Listigen traust!
Viel Schlimmes schuf er uns schon,
doch stets bestrickt er dich wieder.

WOTAN
Wo freier Mut frommt
allein, frag ich nach keinem;
doch des Feindes Neid
zum Nutz sich fügen,
lehrt nur Schlauheit und List,
wie Loge verschlagen sie übt.
Der zum Vertrage mir riet,
versprach mir Freia zu lösen;
auf ihn verlass ich mich nun.

FRICKA
Giants   Und er lässt dich allein.
Dort schreiten rasch
die Riesen heran:
Freia   wo harrt dein schlauer Gehülf?

FREIA
Liebesnot   Wo *har*ren meine
   Brüder,
dass Hilfe sie brächten,
da mein Schwäher die Schwache
verschenkt?
Zu Hilfe, Donner!
Hieher! Hieher!
Rette Freia, mein Froh!

FRICKA
Die in bösem Bund dich
   verrieten,
Giants   sie alle bergen sich *nun.*

FASOLT
Sanft schloss
Schlaf dein Aug;
wir beide bauten
Giants   Schlummers bar die *Burg.*
Mächtger Müh'
müde nie,
stauten starke
Stein wir auf;
steiler Turm,
Tür und Tor,

and fall in his trap!
Much mischief lives in that man;
he fools and flatters you ever.

WOTAN
When strength is called for,
I need no one's assistance;
but to turn men's greed
to my advantage,
that needs wisdom and wit:
and Loge alone is my man.
He who has prompted the pact,
has pledged a ransom for Freia.
I put my faith in his words.

FRICKA
And he won't keep his word.
With giant strides
the giants draw near.
Your artful ally is late.

FREIA
What keeps my thoughtless
    brothers
from coming to help me,
now that Wotan abandons the
    weak?
Come, help me, Donner!
This way! This way!
Save your Freia, my Froh!

FRICKA
First they sponsor ruinous
    bargains,
and then they leave you alone.
[enter Fasolt and Fafner, of gigantic stature
and armed with mighty staves]

FASOLT
Sweet sleep
sealed your eyes
while, never resting,
we have raised your fort.
Plodding on,
never done,
heavy boulders
heap on heap:
towers rose,
portals rose –

Wagner wrote to his friend August
Röckel, 'Make sure you under-
stand Wotan. He resembles us in
all respects.'

The full version of the mighty
Giants motif.

deckt und schliesst
Walhall   im schlanken Schloss den *Saal*.
Dort stehts,
was wir stemmten,
schimmernd hell bescheints
   der Tag:
Giants   zieh nun ein, uns zahl den *Lohn*!

WOTAN
Nennt, Leute, den Lohn:
Treaty   was dünkt euch zu bedingen?

FASOLT
Bedungen ists,
was tauglich uns dünkt;
gemahnt es dich so matt?
Freia   *Freia*, die Holde,
Holda, die Freie,
– vertragen ist's –
sie tragen wir heim.

WOTAN
Seid ihr bei Trost
mit eurem Vertrag?
Denkt auf andern Dank:
Treaty   Freia ist mir nicht feil!

FASOLT

Was sagst du, ha!
Sinnst du Verrat?
Verrat am Vertrag?
Treaty   Die dein *Speer* birgt,
sind sie dir Spiel,
des beratnen Bundes Runen?

FAFNER
Loge   Getreuster Bru*der*!
Merkst du Tropf nun Betrug?

FASOLT
Lichtsohn du,
leicht gefügter,
hör und hüte dich:
Verträgen halte Treu'!
Was du bist,
Treaty   bist du nur durch Ver*träge*;
bedungen ist,

now behold
your mighty mountain home.
Fast holds
what we fashioned;
bravely dawns a bright new
    day.
Enter in and pay the price!

WOTAN
Name, workmen, your wage.
What favours do you fancy?

FASOLT
The fee was fixed;
a fair one it was.
Have you forgot so soon?
Freia, the fair one,
Holda, the free one,
you bartered her;
we bear her away.

Fasolt' s poetic pun, 'Freia, die
Holde, Holda, die Freie', makes use
of Freia's other name, Holda, which
derives from 'hold' (propitious or
fair). The cellos' wistful Freia motif
at this point indicates Fasolt's lyrical
nature.

WOTAN
Be not such fools:
a bargain indeed!
Ask for something else;
Freia is not for sale.

FASOLT [utterly amazed and momentarily
speechless]
What is this? What?
Breaking your word?
Betraying our trust?
What your spear spells,
is it mere sport,
all those runes for trust and
    treaties?

Wotan's spear, symbol of his
authority, counterbalances
Alberich's ring. Both were
obtained by raping nature: the
spear was cut from the World Ash
Tree, the ring from the Rhinegold.

FAFNER
My trustful brother,
fool, to fall for his tricks!

The full Loge motif will not be heard
until Loge's appearance. Here, Fafner's words are accompanied by a
greatly thinned-out Loge motif,
played by the violas, hinting at Loge
as the co-author of the treaty.

FASOLT
Son of light,
light of justice,
listen and beware:
to treaties be you true!
What you are,
you are only by treaties;
and bound by rules,

We read in Homer's *Iliad* that
Troy's walls were built by Apollo
and Poseidon, who were cheated
out of their rewards.

wohl bedacht deine Macht.
Bist weiser du
als witzig wir sind,
bandest uns Freie
zum Frieden du:
all deinem Wissen fluch ich,
fliehe weit deinem Frieden,

Troth   *weisst* du nicht offen,
ehrlich und frei,
Verträgen zu wahren die Treu!
Ein dummer Riese
rät dir das;

Troth   du Weiser, wiss es von *ihm*!

WOTAN
Wie schlau für Ernst du achtest,
was wir zum Scherz nur
    beschlossen.
Die liebliche Göttin,
licht und leicht,
was taugt euch Tölpeln ihr Reiz?

FASOLT
Höhnst du uns?
Ha! wie unrecht!

Freia   Die ihr durch *Schön*heit herrscht,
schimmernd hehres Geschlecht,
wie töricht strebt ihr

Walhall   nach *Tür*men von Stein,
setzt um Burg und Saal

Liebe-Tragik   *Weib*es Wonne zum Pfand!

Giants   Wir *Plump*en
plagen uns
schwitzend mit schwieliger
    Hand,

Freia   ein *Weib* zu gewinnen,
das wonnig und mild
bei uns Armen wohne:

Freia   und verkehrt nennst du den *Kauf*?

FAFNER
Schweig dein faules Schwatzen;
Gewinn werben wir nicht.
Freias Haft
hilft wenig;
doch viel gilts,
den Göttern sie zu entreissen.

Golden Apples   *Gold*ne Äpfel
wachsen in ihrem Garten;

there are bounds to your reach.
You may be wise,
and we may be slow.
Freely we promised
to pledge our peace.
But I shall curse your cunning,
peace be no more between us,
will you not fairly,
honest and free
be true to your barter and bond.
A prattling giant
speaks these words.
You, wise one, listen and learn!

WOTAN
How sly to take in earnest
bargains agreed for
    amusement.
This goddess is lovely,
fair and lithe:
her beauty is not for brutes!

FASOLT
Mocking us?
How demeaning!
You who by beauty reign,
boastful, radiant race,
like fools you dream
of a fortress of stone,
give for wall and hall
grace of woman in pawn.
We plodders
plagued ourselves
slogging with drudge-hardened
    hands,
to win us a woman
who, handsome and mild,
should share our poor homestead.
Will you now call off the deal?

FAFNER
Cease your idle chatter;
no good is to be gained.
She herself
means little,
but why not
deprive the gods of her godhead?
Golden apples
Grow in the goddess's garden.

Wotan denies he had ever intended his proposal to be taken seriously. The bargain was 'agreed for amusement'. He is like Shylock, who in *The Merchant of Venice* said that he had bargained the pound of flesh 'in merry sport'.

Note the explosive sounds of 'Wir Plumpen plagen uns', hinting at the giants as stonemasons.

In Greek mythology Hercules went in search of the golden apples which were guarded by the Hesperides, personifications of clouds gilded by the sun. He crossed the sea in a golden ship, killed a guardian dragon and seized the apples, which were later returned to the Hesperides.

sie allein
weiss die Äpfel zu pflegen;
der Frucht Genuss
frommt ihren Sippen
zu ewig nie
alternder Jugend;
siech und bleich
doch sinkt ihre Blüte,
alt und schwach
schwinden sie hin,
müssen Freia sie missen.

Giants + Golden Apples Ihrer Mitte drum sei sie ent*führt*!

WOTAN
Loge säumt zu lang!

FASOLT
Giants *Schlicht* gib uns Bescheid!

WOTAN
Sinnt auf andern Sold!

FASOLT
Giants Kein *and*rer: Freia allein!

FAFNER
Du da, folge uns!

FREIA
Golden Apples Helft! helft vor den Harten!

FROH
Zu mir, Freia!
Meide sie, Frecher!
Froh schützt die Schöne.

DONNER
Fasolt und Fafner,
fühltet ihr schon
meines Hammers harten Schlag?

FAFNER
Was soll das Drohn?

FASOLT
Giants Was dringst du *her*?

She alone
has the talent to tend them.
The taste thereof
grants to her kinsfolk
an ageless life,
youth everlasting.
Sick and dazed,
the gods would be done for,
their own age
wastes them away,
once fair Freia should fail them.
Therefore let her be plucked from
  their midst!

WOTAN
Loge takes his time.

FASOLT
Quick, make up your mind!

WOTAN
Ask some other prize.

FASOLT
No other, Freia alone!

FAFNER
You there, come with us! [advancing
towards Freia, as Donner and Froh arrive]

FREIA
Help! Beat off those ruffians!

FROH [clasps Freia in his arms]
To me, Freia!
Loose her, you villain!
Froh shields his fair one.

DONNER
Fasolt and Fafner,
do you remember
my hammer's massive might?

FAFNER
Why threaten us?

FASOLT
Why interfere?

In Chinese mythology Queen
Mother Wang provided the gods
with peaches from the tree of
immortality.

Alberich is not the only worshipper
of gold. The gods need it too, and
since it is edible, they require a
constant supply.

The brothers are quite dissimilar.
Fasolt is jovial, trusting and fair-
minded, while Fafner is covetous,
crude and calculating.

As Froh enters, the Golden Apples
motif is rhythmically transformed.
Its character is now more determined, more masculine, since
Froh is Freia's brother.

Kampf kiesten wir nicht,
verlangen nur unsren Lohn.

DONNER
Schon oft zahlt ich
Riesen den Zoll.
Kommt her! des Lohnes Last

Treaty wäg ich mit gutem Gewicht!

WOTAN
Halt, du Wilder!
Nichts durch Gewalt!
Verträge schützt
meines Speeres Schaft:

Freia spar deines Hammers Heft!

FREIA
Grief Wehe! *Wehe*!
Wotan verlässt mich!

FRICKA
Begreif ich dich noch,
Loge grausamer Mann?

WOTAN
Endlich, Loge!
Eiltest du so,
den du geschlossen,
den schlimmen Handel zu
Loge schlicht*en*?

LOGE
Wie? welchen Handel
hätt' ich geschlossen?
Wohl was mit den Riesen
Walhall dort im Rate du *dangst*?
Zu Tiefen und Höhen
treibt mich mein Hang;
Haus und Herd
behagt mir nicht;
Donner und Froh,
die denken an Dach und Fach;
wollen sie frein,
ein Haus muss sie erfreun;
ein stolzer Saal,
ein starkes Schloss,
Walhall danach stand Wotans *Wunsch*.
Haus und Hof,
Saal und Schloss,

Strife's not what we seek.
We only want our wage.

DONNER [swings his hammer]
Once more will I
settle your wage.
This hammer shall bestow
bountiful measure and more.

WOTAN [holds out his spear]
Hold, you hothead!
Nothing by force!
All bonds abide
by my sacred spear.
Strike not a single blow!

FREIA
Break my heart, then;
Wotan forsakes me.

FRICKA
Is this what you want,
merciless man?

WOTAN
Here comes Loge.
Such is your haste,
such your good faith,
when it's time to mend your bad
    bargain?

LOGE [ascending from the valley]
What? I did never
strike any bargain.
That bond with the giants,
you arranged it yourself.
To hollow and height
my fancy will fly.
Home and hearth
I leave alone.
Donner and Froh,
they dream of retreat and rest.
Were they to wed,
they needs must have a house.
A lofty hall,
a lordly home,
such are now Wotan's needs.
House and hall,
rock and roof,

die selige Burg,
sie steht nun stark gebaut;
das Prachtgemäuer
prüft ich selbst;
ob alles fest
forsch ich genau:
Fasolt und Fafner
fand ich bewährt:

Loge kein Stein wankt im Ge*stemm*.
Nicht müssig war ich,
wie mancher hier:
der lügt, wer lässig mich schilt!

WOTAN
Arglistig

Loge *weichst* du mir aus.
Mich zu betrügen
hüte in Treuen dich wohl!
Von allen Göttern
dein einzger Freund,
nahm ich dich auf
in der übel trauenden
   Tross.

Treaty Nun red and rate klug!
Da einst die Bauer der Burg

Loge zum Dank Freia be*dang*en,
du weisst, nicht anders
willigt ich ein,
als weil auf Pflicht du gelobtest

Loge zu lösen das hehre *Pfand.*

LOGE
Mit höchster Sorge
drauf zu sinnen,
wie es zu lösen,

Loge das – hab ich gelobt:
doch dass ich fände,
was nie sich fügt,
was nie gelingt,

Loge wie liess sich das wohl geloben?

FRICKA
Sieh, welch trugvollem
Schelm du getraut!

FROH
Loge heisst du,
doch nenn ich dich Lüge!

your blissful abode,
it stands secure and sound.
The noble pile
I probed with care.
Yes, all is firm,
fine to behold.
Fasolt and Fafner
honoured their word:
each stone stable and stout.
Not idle was I,
like others here.
He lies, who says I was lax.

WOTAN
Slyly you
slip from my grasp.
If you betray me,
I'll make you pay for your tricks.
The gods despise you,
but I do not.
I took you up,
when the others showed their
    contempt.
Keep faith and be my guide!
When they who built me the fort
would ask Freia for bounty,
you know the reason
why I agreed:
because you gave me your promise
to ransom my priceless pledge.

LOGE
With greatest care
to plot and ponder
how to redeem her,
that I undertook.
But how to find
what can not be found,
nor ever will,
how could I keep such a promise?

FRICKA
What a treacherous
traitor he is!

FROH
Loge, listen:
your new name is Liar!

Loge, the fire god, has thoroughly
examined the structure of Wotan's
new fortress: 'The noble pile I
probed with care.' But this is
ominous. To survey one's house,
one would scarcely employ a
potential arsonist.

DONNER
Verfluchte Lohe,
dich lösch ich aus!

LOGE
Ihre Schmach zu decken
schmähen mich Dumme.

WOTAN
In Frieden lasst mir den Freund!
Nicht kennt ihr Loges Kunst:
reicher wiegt
seines Rates Wert,
zahlt er zögernd ihn aus.

Giants   **FAFNER**
Nichts gezögert!
Rasch gezahlt!

FASOLT
Loge   Lang währts mit dem Lohn.

WOTAN
Jetzt hör, Störrischer!
halte Stich!
Wo schweiftest du hin und her?

LOGE
Immer ist Undank
Loges Lohn!
Um dich nur besorgt
sah ich mich um,
durchstöbert im Sturm
Loge   alle Winkel der Welt,
Ersatz für Freia zu suchen,
wie er den Riesen wohl recht.
Umsonst sucht ich
und sehe nun wohl,
in der Welten Ring
nichts ist so reich,
als Ersatz zu muten dem Mann
Liebe-Tragik   für *Weibe*s Wonne und
     Wert.
So weit Leben und Weben,
in Wasser, Erd und Luft,
viel frug ich,
forschte bei allen,
wo Kraft nur sich rührt

DONNER
Accursed Fire,
I'll choke your flames.

LOGE
Just to save their blushes,
boobies rebuke me. [Donner and Froh
threaten Loge]

WOTAN
Offend not Wotan's own friend,
but learn his ways and wiles!
Apt advice
flows from Loge's lips.
Patient waiting will pay.

FAFNER
No more waiting!
Promptly pay!

Fafner puns on Wotan's 'zahlt er
zögernd', giving both waiting and
paying more immediate relevance.

FASOLT
We want our reward!

WOTAN
Come here, wilful one,
keep your word!
Why did you linger so long?

LOGE
Insults are always
Loge's lot.
For your sake alone
looked I around,
relentlessly ransacked
the ends of the earth,
to find a ransom for Freia,
fit for the giants' content.
I delved vainly,
and now I declare:
in the whole wide world
nothing compares
in the hearts and senses of men,
with Woman's sweetness and
  grace.
Where life urges and surges,
in water, earth and air,
there searched I,
searched for an answer,
from those who are strong

Loge's lengthy narration is a
celebration of Love. The staggered
entries of the string instruments,
from the lowest to the highest,
lighten and brighten the precari-
ous situation. No wonder the
gods are spellbound.

		und Keime sich regen,
	Freia	was wohl dem *Manne* mächtger dünkt
Liebe-Tragik	*Freia*	als *Weib*es Wonne und Wert?

Doch so weit Leben und Weben,
verlacht nur ward
meine fragende List:
in Wasser, Erd' und Luft
lassen will nichts
von Lieb und Weib.
Nur einen sah ich,

	Rhinegold	der sagte der Liebe *ab*: um rotes Gold
	Joy	entriet er des Weibes Gunst.

Des Rheines klare Kinder
klagten mir ihre Not:
der Nibelung,
Nacht-Alberich,

	Innocence	*buhl*te vergebens um der Badenden Gunst;
	Rhinegold	das Rheingold da
	Ring	raubte sich rächend der Dieb:

das dünkt ihm nun
das teuerste Gut,

Liebe-Tragik	*Grief*	*hehr*er als Weibes Huld.

Um den gleissenden Tand,
der Tiefe entwandt,
erklang mir der Töchter
   Klage:
an dich, Wotan,
wenden sie sich,
dass zu Recht du zögest den
   Räuber,

	Rhinegold	*das* Gold dem Wasser wieder gebest,
	Joy	und ewig es bliebe ihr Eigen.

Dir's zu melden

	Loge	gelobt ich den *Mäd*chen: nun löste Loge sein Wort.

WOTAN
Törig bist du,
wenn nicht gar tückisch!
Mich selbst siehst du in Not:
wie hülf ich andren zum Heil?

and those who are tender,
what does the heart
of man prefer
to Woman's sweetness and grace?
[all stand in amazement]
But where life urges and surges,
derided was
all my cunning request:
in water, earth and air,
none would relinquish
Woman's love.
But one man only,
he did turn away from love.
For blood-red gold
he hounded love from his heart.
The Rhine's fair, gentle children
cried to me in their need.
The Nibelung,
Night-Alberich,
vainly endeavoured
to win favour and love.
The Rhinegold then
stole he instead in revenge,
and now it seems
more worthy to him,
greater than Woman's grace.
For their treasure divine,
now plucked from the Rhine,
the maidens make much
   lamenting.
To you, Wotan,
would they appeal:
let your judgement fall on the
   felon,
return the Rhinegold
to the waters,
and let it repose there for ever.
This to tell you
I promised the maidens.
So Loge did keep his word!

WOTAN
Are you blind,
or simply vindictive?
Perplexed am I myself;
how could I comfort those maids?

Loge reports what we have already witnessed in Scene 1. It is, however, news to the gods, and spectators welcome the second hearing, as they welcome the recapitulation section in a symphonic movement.

The Forge motif of Scene 3 is anticipated in Loge's words 'Um den gleissenden Tand' ('Tand ... entwandt' – one of Wagner's rare rhymes). The Rhinemaidens' 'treasure divine, now plucked from the Rhine' is indeed being hammered and forged even now, by Alberich's slaves in Nibelheim.

Loge acts for Wotan and for the Rhinemaidens, but he is not just a double agent. He is everybody's agent if hired. Hence his flickering, elusive, chromatic music.

The sudden shift to C major marks the appearance of the Rhinegold motif, as Loge ends his report by advising Wotan to restore the gold to the Rhine. Wagner gives the direction 'with increasing warmth' to the singer. Loge's warning springs from his genuine concern.

FASOLT
Nicht gönn ich das Gold dem Alben;
viel Not schon schuf uns der
    Niblung,
doch schlau entschlüpfte
unsrem Zwange immer der Zwerg.

FAFNER
Neue Neidtat
sinnt uns der Niblung,

Loge gibt das Gold ihm *Macht*.
Du da, Loge!
Sag ohne Lug:
was Grosses gilt denn das Gold,
dass dem Niblung es genügt?

Joy LOGE
Ein Tand ists
in des Wassers Tiefe,

Ring lachenden Kindern zur Lust;
doch, ward es zum runden
Reife geschmiedet,
hilft es zur höchsten Macht,
gewinnt dem Manne die Welt.

WOTAN
Von des Rheines Gold
hört ich raunen:
Beute-Runen
berge sein roter Glanz,
Macht und Schätze
schüf' ohne Mass ein Reif.

FRICKA
Taugte wohl
des goldnen Tandes
gleissend Geschmeid
auch Frauen zu schönem
    Schmuck?

LOGE
Des Gatten Treu
ertrotzte die Frau,

Enchantment *trüge* sie hold
den hellen Schmuck,

Forge den schimmernd *Zwerg*e
    schmieden,
rührig im Zwange des Reifs.

FASOLT
The gold I begrudge the Niblung;
much harm he's done us
    already;
but he is artful
and he always slips through our
    hands.

FAFNER
Yet more mischief
will he be up to,
now he's gained the gold.
You there, Loge,
speak and don't lie!
What does he see in the gold,
that it satisfies his greed?

LOGE
A plaything
in the placid waters,
cheering and charming the maids;
but when to a golden
ring it is rounded,
then is it nonpareil
and wins its owner the world.

WOTAN
Of the gold's repute
I heard rumours:
runes of riches
gleam in the glowing gold.
Boundless power
would such a ring bestow.

FRICKA [to Loge]
Do you think,
such golden garnish,
such dainty delight,
be fit for the wife of my lord?

LOGE
No husband would
forsake his own wife,
were she to choose
some dazzling charm,
which dwarfs below are
    forging,
ruled by the lord of the ring.

During the exchange between
Loge and Wotan, the Ring motif is
heard ten times in succession.
The effect is hypnotic. Under its
spell Wotan is ready to contemplate illegal action. Even Fricka is
prepared to connive.

FRICKA *Freia*
Gewänne mein Gatte
sich wohl das Gold?

WOTAN *Rhinegold*
Des Reifes zu walten,
rätlich will es mich dünken.
Doch wie, Loge,
lernt ich die Kunst?
Wie schüf' ich mir das Geschmeid?

LOGE
Ein *Run*enzauber *Ring*
zwingt das Gold zum Reif;
keiner kennt ihn;
doch *ein*er übt ihn leicht, *Liebe-Tragik*
der selger Lieb' entsagt.
Das sparst du wohl;
zu spät auch kämst du:
Alberich zauderte nicht,
*zagl*os gewann er des Zaubers *Ring*
    Macht:
*gerat*en ist ihm der Ring! *Liebe-Tragik*

DONNER
Zwang uns allen
schüfe der Zwerg,
würd' ihm der Reif nicht entrissen.

WOTAN
Den Ring muss ich haben!

FROH
Leicht erringt
ohne *Liebe*sfluch er sich jetzt. *Liebe-Tragik*

LOGE
Spottleicht,
ohne Kunst wie im Kinderspiel.

WOTAN
So rate, wie?

LOGE
Durch Raub!
Was ein Dieb stahl,
das stiehlst du dem Dieb:
ward leichter ein Eigen erlangt? *Loge*
Doch mit arger Wehr

FRICKA [to Wotan]
Perchance my dear husband
harvests the gold?

WOTAN
That ring should be my ring;
handy were it and helpful.
But how, Loge?
Counsel me, how!
What force will fashion the ring?

LOGE
A magic cypher
rounds the golden ring.
None may know it
but he, who would let go
of all delights of love.
That's not for you!
You are too late now;
Alberich acted in time,
boldly unlocking the magic
    code:
and he is the lord of the ring!

DONNER
He would lord it
over us all,
unless the ring can be captured.

WOTAN
That ring shall be ravished!

FROH
Yes, indeed!
and no need for giving up love.

LOGE
Quite so.
It were child's play to reap the ring.

WOTAN
Then tell us how!

LOGE
By theft!
What a thief stole,
you steal from the thief.
You gather your goods just like that.
But on grimmest guard

Wotan means to hold the ring as
a deterrent. He conveniently for-
gets his original intention: the
gold was to ransom Freia.

Rhinegold	*wahrt* sich Alberich;
Ring	*klug* und fein
	musst du verfahren,
	ziehst du den Räuber zu Recht,
Joy	um des *Rheine*s Töchtern
	den roten Tand,
	das Gold, wieder zu geben:
Rhinegold	*denn* darum flehen sie dich.

Joy WOTAN
Des Rheines Töchtern?
Was taugt mir der Rat!

Innocence FRICKA
Von dem Wassergezücht
mag ich nichts wissen:
schon manchen Mann,
mir zum Leid,
verlockten sie buhlend im Bad.

Freia FAFNER
Glaub mir, mehr als Freia
frommt das gleissende Gold;
auch ew'ge Jugend erjagt,
wer durch Goldes Zauber sie
Golden Apples   *zwingt.*

Rhinegold   *Crisis*   *Giants*
Hör, Wotan,
der Harrenden Wort:
Freia bleib euch in Frieden;
leichtern Lohn
fand ich zur Lösung:
uns rauhen Riesen genügt
Ring des *Nib*lungen rotes Gold.

WOTAN
Seid ihr bei Sinn?
Was nicht ich besitze,
soll ich euch Schamlosen
   schenken?

Giants FAFNER
Schwer baute
Walhall dort sich die *Burg*:
leicht wirds dir
mit listger Gewalt
(was im Neidspiel nie uns gelang)
Loge den Niblungen fest zu fahn.

is our Alberich.
Take great care,
plotting the plunder;
then give the devil his due.
Grant the Rhine's fair daughters
their golden joy,
to rest deep in the river.
The maidens hope for your help.

WOTAN
The Rhine's fair daughters?
What are they to me?

FRICKA
Of that billowy brood
speak not to Fricka,
for many men,
sad to say,
they lured to their watery lair.

FAFNER [to Fasolt]
Better far than Freia
were that glittering gold.
Eternal youth would be ours,
were the magic gold in our grasp.
[Fasolt agrees unwillingly. Fafner turns
to Wotan.]
Hear, Wotan,
our mind is made up.
Freia shall have her freedom.
Lesser prize
pay to redeem her:
we friendless fellows accept
the Nibelung's garish gold.

WOTAN
Are you insane?
The gold is not mine yet.
Shame on your greedy ambition!

FAFNER
Hard toil
raised towers for you.
Now call on
your crafty control,
(you command it better than we)
to gather the Niblung's gold.

Wagner does not substantiate
Fricka's allegation. We are left to
wonder whether she knows more
than we do, or whether she
thinks of the 'billowy brood', by
their very nature, as loose
women. After all, she is the
guardian goddess of holy
matrimony.

Cellos play a chromatically distorted
Freia motif, robbing it of its earlier
sensual appeal. This is how the
opportunist Fafner hears it.

The gold has appreciated in value.
'Ewige Jugend' (eternal youth) is
the new added bonus.

WOTAN
Für euch müht' ich
mich um den Alben?
Für euch fing ich den Feind?
Unverschämt
und überbegehrlich
macht euch Dumme mein Dank!

FASOLT
Hieher, Maid!
in unsre Macht!
Als Pfand folgst du uns jetzt,
bis wir Lösung empfahn.

FREIA
Wehe! Wehe! Weh!

FAFNER
Fort von hier

Treaty   sei sie entführt!
Bis Abend, achtets wohl,
pflegen wir sie als Pfand:
wir kehren wieder;
doch kommen wir,

Ring   und be*reit* liegt nicht als Lösung
das Rheingold licht und rot –

FASOLT
Zu End ist die Frist dann,
Freia verfallen;
für immer folge sie uns!

FREIA
Schwester! Brüder!
Rettet! helft!

LOGE
Über Stock und Stein zu Tal
stapfen sie hin;
durch des Rheines Wasser-
    flut
waten die Riesen:
fröhlich nicht
hängt Freia
den Rauhen über dem Rücken!
Heia! hei!
Wie taumeln die Tölpel dahin!
Durch das Tal talpen sie schon:

WOTAN
For you should I
meddle with Alberich?
For you fetter the foe?
Shameless creatures,
do not provoke me
with your monstrous demands!

FASOLT [seizes Freia]
Come here, maid!
You are our prize,
our pledge, hostage and bond,
till your ransom is paid.

FREIA
Help me! Help me! Help!

FAFNER
Far from here
shall she be borne.
Till nightfall, mark my words,
she has nothing to fear.
We shall return then,
but if you fail
and the Rhinegold is not ready,
our rosy ransom, then –

FASOLT
– then time will be up,
and Freia is forfeit.
Then Freia's ours to enjoy.

FREIA
Sister! Brothers!
Save me! Help! [she is dragged away by
the giants]

LOGE
Up the rocky road, down dale
they plod, lurching along.
Through the Rhine's deep waters
   now
waddle the giants.
Freia hangs,
far from happy,
across the clodhoppers' shoulders.
Heia! hei!
Those ruffians are rolling along!
Through the vale see them push on.

wohl an Riesenheims Mark
erst halten sie Rast!
Was sinnt nun Wotan so
   wild?

Freia   Den selgen Göttern wie *gehts*?

Trügt mich ein Nebel?

Golden Apples   Neckt mich ein *Traum*?

Freia   Wie bang und *bleich*
verblüht ihr so bald!
Euch erlischt der Wangen

Golden Apples   *Licht*;
der Blick eures Auges verblitzt!

Frisch, mein Froh,
noch ists ja früh!
Deiner Hand, Donner,
entsinkt ja der Hammer!
Was ists mit Fricka?
Freut sie sich wenig
ob Wotans grämlichem Grau,
das schier zum Greisen ihn

Freia   schafft?

FRICKA

Grief   *We*he! Wehe!
Was ist geschehn?

DONNER
Mir sinkt die Hand.

FROH
Mir stockt das Herz.

Golden Apples   LOGE
Jetzt fand ichs: hört, was euch fehlt!
Von Freias Frucht
genosset ihr heute noch nicht:
die goldnen Äpfel
in ihrem Garten,
sie machten euch tüchtig und jung,
asst ihr sie jeden Tag.
Des Gartens Pflegerin
ist nun verpfändet;
an den Ästen darbt
und dorrt das Obst,

Loge   bald fällt faul es herab.
Mich kümmerts minder;

Soon at Riesenheim's bounds
will they draw breath. [to the gods]
What brooding clouds Wotan's
    brow?
The eternal gods look so old!
[mist fills the stage, giving the gods an aged
aspect]
Vapours delude me;
dream world, away!
How weak you seem,
wrinkled and worn!
From your cheeks the bloom has
    fled,
the blaze of your eyes has grown
    dim.
Courage, Froh,
young is the day!
Mind your hand, Donner,
you're dropping the hammer!
What's up with Fricka?
Is she unhappy
that Wotan's grizzled and grey,
an old man ahead of his time?

FRICKA
Sorrow! Sorrow!
What's going on?

DONNER
My hand grows weak.

FROH
My heart stands still.

LOGE
I have it! This is what ails you:
of Freia's fruit
you have not tasted today.
The golden apples
that grow in her garden,
provide you with vigour and youth,
thanks to an apple a day.
The garden's guardian,
she has been bartered,
and the apples rot
and fade away,
and soon they'll hit the ground.
Not that I'm worried.

The *pianissimo* tremolo on the
strings suggests the sudden age-
ing of the gods.

an mir ja kargte
Freia von je
knausernd die köstliche Frucht:
denn halb so echt nur
bin ich wie, Herrliche, ihr!
Doch ihr setztet alles
auf das jüngende Obst:
das wussten die Riesen wohl;
auf euer Leben legten sie's an:

Golden Apples nun sorgt, wie ihr das wahrt!
Ohne die Äpfel
alt und grau, greis und
  grämlich,
welkend zum Spott aller Welt,
erstirbt der Götter Stamm.

FRICKA
Wotan, Gemahl,
unselger Mann!
Sieh, wie dein Leichtsinn
lachend uns allen
Ring Schimpf und Schmach erschuf!

WOTAN
Auf, Loge!
hinab mit mir!
Nach Nibelheim fahren wir
  nieder:
Joy gewinnen will ich das *Gold*.

LOGE
Die Rheintöchter
riefen dich an:
so dürfen Erhörung sie hoffen?

WOTAN
Schweige, Schwätzer!
Freia, die gute,
Freia gilt es zu lösen.

LOGE
Wie du befiehlst
führ ich dich gern:
steil hinab
steigen wir denn durch den Rhein?

To me, dear Freia
always was mean
with the immaculate fruit;
for half as god-like
am I, not true-born like you!
You staked your existence
on those apples of youth;
the giants are well aware
that this would wipe out
    Wotan and all.
Now look to your own lives!
Lost are your apples;
old and grey, shrunk and
    shrivelled,
scolded and scorned by the world,
the gods will be no more.

FRICKA
Wotan, my lord,
ill-fated man!
See how your rashness
brought us derision.
Shame, o bitter shame!

WOTAN
Now, Loge,
come down with me!
To Nibelheim let us dive
    downwards,
for there I'll harvest the gold.

LOGE
The Rhinemaidens
raised their complaint.
Shall Wotan restore them their
    treasure?

WOTAN
Peace, you prattler!
Freia, our loved one,
Freia must be recovered!

LOGE
Just as you wish;
I'll be your guide,
all the way down!
Shall we descend through the Rhine?

Heinrich Porges and Felix Mottl,
Wagner's assistants at the
Bayreuth première of the *Ring* in
1876, report that Loge was
directed to avoid any suggestion
of mockery in the lines 'scolded
and scorned by the world, the
gods will be no more', but rather
to present this 'with great
seriousness'.

WOTAN
Nicht durch den Rhein!

LOGE
So schwingen wir uns
durch die Schwefelkluft:
Loge — dort schlüpfe mit mir hin*ein*!

WOTAN
Ihr andern harrt
bis Abend hier:
verlorner Jugend
Ring *Loge* — er*jag* ich erlösendes *Gold*!

DONNER
Fahre wohl, Wotan!

FROH
Glück auf! Glück auf!

FRICKA
O kehre bald
Loge — zur bangenden *Frau*!

Liebe-Tragik	*Loge*	*Liebe-Tragik*
	Loge	*Liebe-Tragik*
	Liebe-Tragik	*Grief*

WOTAN
Not through the Rhine!

LOGE
Then must we go down
through the sulphur cleft.
Together let us steal in!

WOTAN
You all stand by,
till evening falls.
Our youth that left us,
returns when I rescue the gold.

DONNER
Fare you well, Wotan!

FROH
Good luck! Good luck!

FRICKA
O, soon return
to your sorrowing wife!
[Wotan has followed Loge through the cleft.
Sulphurous vapour fills the stage, becoming
darker and rising from the bottom to the top.
This gives the impression that the stage is
sinking down.]

Wotan's bad conscience forbids
the short route to Nibelheim, via
the Rhine. He might have to face
the Rhinemaidens! The very name
of the alternative route, the 'sulphur cleft', has an ill-omened,
almost diabolic ring.

Wotan sets out to gain Alberich's
ring and golden hoard, not to
make amends to the Rhinemaidens, not to ransom Freia, but to
secure his guardianship of the
world. Norse mythology, Wagner's
source, does not endow Wotan
with either omnipotence or omni-
science. Fate rules gods and men
alike. Wotan is the stage on which
the tragedy of life is played out.

Transition

Wotan is determined to appropriate Alberich's golden treasure. He would then have three options:

1. to restore the gold to the Rhine
2. to ransom Freia
3. to keep the gold

The first option constitutes an act of justice, rectifying Alberich's crime and restoring the original, guiltless state of the world. The second option secures the release of the hostage, without whom the gods would face extinction. The last option could offer both Freia's release and the gods' returning youth, since the treasure includes the all-powerful ring.

Wotan and Loge are about to invade Nibelheim, Home of Vapours which, according to Norse mythology, is the undermost of the nine existing worlds. Alberich, lord of the Nibelungs, has turned his brother Mime into his personal slave. The other Nibelungs only appear as a mass of terrified labourers. Early storytellers seem to have been intrigued by those Nibelungs. The *Volsunga Saga* speaks of a treasure gained by the Gibichungs, who then turned into Nibelungs. According to the *Nibelungenlied*, Siegfried becomes a Nibelung on acquiring the treasure. The Burgundians too, having obtained the hoard, turn into Nibelungs. Such metamorphoses seem to be an occupational hazard of treasure seekers.

The Music: from the Mountain Heights to Nibelheim

The transition from Scene 1 to Scene 2 took us from the depths of the Rhine to the mountain heights. The transition from Scene 2 to Scene 3 takes us from the heights to even lower depths, to the Home of Vapours, Nibelheim. Wagner prescribes 'sulphurous vapours turning into black clouds'. The music is designed to give an impression of 'the stage sinking ever deeper into the earth'. But it also conveys, most powerfully, the joyless life in Alberich's new world. Merely naming the leitmotifs provides a clue to what is in Wagner's mind:

Loge
Liebe-Tragik
Grief
Liebesnot
Rhinegold
Ring
Rhinegold
Forge
Liebesnot
Forge
Grief
Ring

To provide a link with the previous scene, the transition remains initially in E minor, the key in which Scene 2 ended. The Loge motif meanders chromatically, with woodwind gyrating downwards and bassoon, bass clarinet, bass tuba and contrabass tuba upwards, providing a giddy contrary motion. The music then shifts to B flat minor, the key of Alberich's domain, and closely related to the D flat major, Wotan's Walhall key. Again, Wagner is drawing our attention to the link between Wotan and Alberich. Vapours and clouds, incidentally, held unexpected perils for the orchestra at the 1876 Bayreuth performance. They played havoc with the string players' intonation, while their swirling motion created a vicious draught. Wagner sighed, 'Not only did I compose the opera, I also have to close the windows.'

The Liebe-Tragik motif sounds four times in succession, played first by trombones, then by horns – the yearning of imprisoned love. Next we hear the Grief motif, again four times, played by cellos and woodwind in rapid interchange. The Liebesnot motif follows, twelve times, very fast, announced by cellos, followed by violas and finally by violins. A bass trumpet then presents a sombre picture of the Rhinegold motif, which ushers in the strings' Ring motif and, once more, the Rhinegold motif, this time with an added trumpet – pungent reminders of Alberich's trespasses. Meanwhile, the full orchestra has begun its relentless *fortissimo* Forge rhythm, which threatens to drown the trumpets' Liebesnot motif: in Nibelheim love is being hammered to death. The Forge motif is now taken over by eighteen anvils, off-stage. Wagner is extraordinarily precise in his instructions:

9 small anvils: right, left and background
2 large anvils: right, but not close together
2 large anvils: left, but not close together
2 large anvils: background, but not close together
1 very large anvil: background
1 very large anvil: right
1 very large anvil: left

A glance at the score shows Wagner's attention to the minutest detail in creating the required sound, which was to combine a picture of ceaseless labour and soulless existence:

As the anvils gradually grow less menacing, the Grief motif is sounded seven times in succession by bassoons, cellos and double basses. Finally, there is a frenzied sequence of incomplete Ring motifs (only down, not up again), played by the strings, presenting the veritable goldrush which leads into the third scene.

Alberich; illustration by
Maxfield Parrish (1894)

Loge pretends to be frightened of
Alberich in disguise as a dragon;
illustration by Arthur Rackham (1910)

3
Scene

Synopsis
Leitmotifs
Libretto

Scene 3: Story

Nibelheim

Mime, compelled by Alberich, has forged the Tarnhelm, a magic cap which can render its wearer invisible, transport him with lightning speed, or transform him into somebody or something else. Mime's attempt to keep the Tarnhelm for himself is brutally thwarted by Alberich.

Wotan and Loge arrive, and find Mime lamenting Alberich's cruelty towards himself and his fellow Nibelungs.

Alberich appears, driving his workers before him. He sees himself as the future ruler of the world, and he predicts his eventual ascendancy over Wotan and all his gods.

Loge coaxes Alberich into demonstrating the Tarnhelm's magic power. Easily duped, Alberich turns himself first into a huge serpent, and then into a tiny toad. Wotan steps on the creature, who is re-transformed into Alberich. Loge ties him up and, together with Wotan, conveys him to the upper region.

Alberich is captured by Wotan and Loge; scenic design by Joseph Hoffman, Bayreuth 1876

Scene 3: Action

1. Alberich demands the Tarnhelm from Mime
2. Mime maltreated
3. Alberich revels in his power
4. Orchestra: Nibelheim rampant
5. Mime complains to Wotan and Loge
6. Alberich as slave-driver
7. Loge goads Alberich
8. Alberich's picture of the future
9. Loge sets his trap
10. Serpent transformation
11. Toad transformation
12. Alberich captured
13. Orchestra: from Nibelheim to the heights

Loge: 'Up with our quarry!';
Alberich is dragged upwards
by Wotan and Loge.

Scene 3: Leitmotifs

The leitmotifs new to the scene follow in chronological order, together with the page number of first appearance.

Tarnhelm   p.106

Gold's Dominion   p.116

Treasure   p.118

Arrogance   p.120

Dragon   p.124

Commentary on the Leitmotifs

Tarnhelm

This sequence of palpitating minor chords, played by muted horns at its first appearance, ends in an open fifth, a chord which is neither major nor minor. Like the wearer of the Tarnhelm, it cannot be apprehended.

Gold's Dominion

Rhythmically and melodically related to the Forge motif, it symbolizes Alberich's power proliferating wealth, an aspect which is emphasized by the motif's shift from gloomy minor to exultant major. When first heard, it accompanies Alberich's warning to the slaves: 'Tremble in terror, you harnessed horde, subjects to the ring's great lord!' Wagner's stage direction reads, appropriately, 'they shriek and scatter.'

Treasure

This motif graphically portrays the heaping up of the hoard. 'My envy is hard to contain,' says Loge, while bassoons and bass clarinet lend the motif a grisly presence.

Arrogance

Cross-breeding the Walhall and Loge motifs creates this hybrid. Loge arrogates Wotan's authority, which he tinges with his own brand of buffoonery. Wind instruments and horns play a rapid, somewhat undignified snatch of the Walhall motif which merges into a flicker of the Loge motif, ending with an impudent trill.

Dragon

Fittingly, this motif is closely related to the Treasure motif. In *Siegfried* Fafner transforms himself into a dragon and guards his treasure by sleeping upon it. At the motif's first appearance bass tubas and contrabass tuba suggest a horrifying monster, more formidable than the usual stage monstrosity.

3. Szene

ALBERICH
Hehe! hehe!
Hieher! hieher!

Alberich Tückischer Zwerg!
Tapfer gezwickt
sollst du mir sein,
schaffst du nicht fertig,
wie ich's bestellt,
zur Stund das feine Geschmeid!

MIME
Ohe! Ohe!
Au! Au!
Lass mich nur los!
Fertig ist's,
wie du befahlst;
mit Fleiss und Schweiss
ist es gefügt:
nimm nur die Nägel vom Ohr!

ALBERICH
Was zögerst du dann
und zeigst es nicht?

MIME
Ich Armer zagte,
dass noch was fehle.

ALBERICH
Was wär' noch nicht fertig?

MIME
Hier ... und da.

ALBERICH
Was hier und da?

Scene 3

[Nibelheim: subterranean cavern. Alberich drags Mime out of a shaft at the side.]

ALBERICH
Come here, I say!
Come here to me!
Treacherous troll!
Drubbing and clouts
shall be your doom,
if you should fail
to finish on time
the helm, the delicate helm!

Alberich calls his brother 'treacherous troll'. Pot and kettle.

MIME
O help! O help!
Au! Au!
Do let me go!
All is done,
as you decreed.
I sweated blood,
moulding the thing.
Brother, stop mauling my ear!

ALBERICH
Then why the delay?
Produce it now!

MIME
Poor Mime's worried:
something is wanting.

ALBERICH
And what should be wanting?

MIME
Here – and there –

ALBERICH
What here and there?

Her das Geschmeid!

Tarnhelm

Schau, du Schelm!
Alles geschmiedet
und fertig gefügt,
wie ich's befahl!
So wollte der Tropf
schlau mich betrügen,
für sich behalten
das hehre Geschmeid,
das meine List
ihn zu schmieden gelehrt?

Tarnhelm Kenn ich dich dummen Dieb?

Dem Haupt fügt sich der Helm:
ob sich der Zauber auch zeigt?

'Nacht und Nebel,
niemand gleich!'

Siehst du mich, Bruder?

MIME

Alberich Wo bist du? Ich sehe dich nicht.

ALBERICH

Grief So fühle mich doch,
du fauler Schuft!
Nimm das für dein Diebsgelüst!

MIME
Ohe! Ohe!

Grief *Au*! Au!

ALBERICH
Haha haha haha!
Hab Dank, du Dummer!
Dein Werk bewährt sich gut.

Grief Hoho! Hoho!
Niblungen all,
neigt euch nun Alberich!
Überall weilt er nun,
euch zu bewachen;
Ruh und Rast
ist euch zerronnen;

Ring *ihm* müsst ihr schaffen,
wo nicht ihr ihn schaut;

Hand me the thing! [the terrified Mime
drops a piece of metal work]
Look, you crook!
All has been fitted
and carefully forged
after my plan.
A curse on the clown,
trying to trick me,
to keep the sterling
stuff for himself,
which without me
he could never have made.
Fool, have I found you out? [he places
the Tarnhelm on his head]
The helm over my head!
Now will the magic be mine? [very
softly]
'Night and vapours:
I'm no more!' [he vanishes in a column of
vapour]
Brother, where am I?

MIME
Where are you? I can't make you
    out!

ALBERICH [invisible]
Yes, brother, you can,
you lazy lout!
Take this for your grudging greed!
[he scourges Mime]

MIME
Let go! Let go!
Au! Au!

ALBERICH [still invisible]
Haha haha haha!
I thank you, thickhead!
Your labour serves me well.
Hoho! Hoho!
Niblungen all,
bow down to Alberich!
Everywhere looms he now,
prying and spying.
No more peace,
leisure or pleasure.
He is your guard,
your invisible will.

Muted horns playing the Tarnhelm
motif produce a magical, other-
worldly effect.

In *The Perfect Wagnerite*, Shaw
wrote: 'This helmet is a very com-
mon article in our streets ... it makes
a man invisible as a shareholder,
and changes him into ... a bene-
factor of the poor ... when he is
really a parasite of the common-
wealth, consuming a great deal and
producing nothing.'

Loge, lord of chromatic ambiguity,
lurks in the Tarnhelm motif.

Alberich wonders whether the Tarnhelm will prove effective: 'Now will
the magic be mine?' Since he cannot tell whether he is indeed invisible, he seeks confirmation from
Mime.

The realistic trouncing music that
accompanies Alberich's words
results from the mixture of the
Alberich and Grief motifs, snarled by
the strings.

Plato tells of Gyges, King of the Lydi-
ans, who descended into the under-
world and obtained a ring which
rendered him invisible – Wagner's
ring and Tarnhelm in one.

There are several ways of amassing
riches, such as calculating slyness or
brutal possessiveness. Mime
embodies the former, Alberich the
latter.

wo nicht ihr ihn gewahrt,
seid seiner gewärtig:
untertan seid ihr ihm immer!
Hoho! Hoho!
Hört, er naht:
der Niblungen Herr!

Forge
Grief
Loge

LOGE
Nibelheim hier:
durch bleiche Nebel
Forge was blitzen dort feurige *Funk*en!

MIME
Grief *Au*! Au! Au!

WOTAN
Hier stöhnt es laut:
was liegt im Gestein?

LOGE
Was Wunder wimmerst du hier?

MIME
Grief *Oh*e! Ohe!
Au! Au!

LOGE
Hei, Mime! Muntrer Zwerg!
Was zwickt und zwackt dich denn
  so?

MIME
Lass mich in Frieden!

LOGE
Das will ich freilich,
und mehr noch, hör:
helfen will ich dir, Mime!

MIME
Wer hälfe mir?
Gehorchen muss ich
dem leiblichen Bruder,
der mich in Bande gelegt.

He has ten thousand eyes,
to test your obedience.
You are his creatures for ever!
Hoho! Hoho!
Now he draws near,
the Nibelung lord! [the column of
vapour disappears with Alberich, as Wotan
and Loge descend from a cleft]

LOGE
Nibelheim here!
The murky vapours
are riddled with fiery flashes.

After the relentless repetitions of
the Grief motifs, blared out by brass
and woodwind, it is a relief to hear
the strings greet Loge's arrival.

MIME
Au! Au! Au!

The comparability of Nibelheim with
any nineteenth-century 'satanic mill',
and of the Nibelung slaves with
modern sweated labour, is obvious.

WOTAN
What groans are these?
Who lies on the ground?

LOGE
What have we howling here?

MIME
Ohe! Ohe!
Au! Au!

LOGE
Hi, Mime! dainty dwarf!
What haunts and harrows you
    so?

MIME
Clear off and leave me!

LOGE
Gladly, good fellow,
and what is more,
Help I offer you, Mime!

Listen to the bassoons, accompany-
ing Mime's 'Who could help me?'
Their falling augmented fourths,
repeated several times, are a pre-
echo of the Brooding motif, which is
to play a prominent part in
Siegfried.

MIME
Who could help me?
I must submit
to my merciless brother.
I am his scullion and slave.

LOGE
Dich, Mime, zu binden,
was gab ihm die Macht?

MIME
Mit arger List
schuf sich Alberich
aus Rheines Gold
einen gelben Reif:
seinem starken Zauber
Ring   *zittern* wir staunend;
mit ihm zwingt er uns alle,
Forge   der Niblungen nächt'ges *Heer.*
Sorglose Schmiede,
schufen wir sonst wohl
Schmuck unsern Weibern,
wonnig Geschmeid,
niedlichen Niblungentand,
wir lachten lustig der Müh.
Grief   Nun zwingt uns der *Schlimme,*
in Klüfte zu schlüpfen,
für ihn allein
uns immer zu mühn.
Durch des Ringes Gold
errät seine Gier,
wo neuer Schimmer
in Schachten sich birgt:
da müssen wir spähen,
spüren und graben,
Ring   die Beute schmelzen
und schmieden den Guss,
ohne Ruh und Rast
dem Herrn zu häufen den Hort.

LOGE
Dich Trägen soeben
traf wohl sein Zorn?

MIME
Mich Armen, ach,
Forge   *Tarnhelm*   mich zwang er zum ärgst*en:*
ein Helmgeschmeid
hiess er mich schweissen;
genau befahl er,
wie es zu fügen.
Wohl merkt' ich klug,
welch mächt'ge Kraft
zu eigen dem Werk,
das aus Erz ich wob;

LOGE
But, Mime, what gave him
control over you?

MIME
A shifty snake,
such is Alberich.
He raided the Rhine
for his golden ring.
At its mighty spell
we quave and quiver.
With that ring he can lord it
over Nibelheim's hidden host.
Once we were free,
to work as we wished,
shaped rings for our women,
baubles and toys,
dainty Niblung delight,
and we would sing for joy.
But now he compels us
to creep into caverns,
for him alone
to sweat and to slave.
Through his golden ring
his greed can divine
where ever new riches
are hid in the rocks.
It's there we must ferret,
there we must forage,
and melt the booty,
and make golden bars,
every night and day,
to heap the hoard of our lord!

LOGE
Just now, were you idle?
Was he displeased?

MIME
Poor me, alas,
he holds me in bondage.
A helm of mail
I had to fashion.
Exact commands
he gave for the forging.
I knew full well
what wondrous power
was locked in the helm,
in my handiwork.

The Forge motif, played by a carefree horn, sounds quite cosy as it
recalls the lost golden age of the
Nibelungs. A few bars later, on 'But
now he compels us', cellos and
double basses toll the same motif,
but this time reinforced by low
woodwind shrieking the Grief motif.

'Now I am in Nibelheim. Today
Mime is airing his discontent.'
(Wagner to Liszt, 17 December 1853)

	für mich drum hüten
	wollt' ich den Helm,
	durch seinen Zauber
	Alberichs Zwang mich entziehn –
	vielleicht, ja vielleicht
	den Lästigen selbst überlisten,
	in meine Gewalt ihn zu werfen,
Ring	den *Ring* ihm zu entreissen,
	dass, wie ich Knecht jetzt dem Kühnen,
Ring + Forge	mir Freien er selber dann *frön'*!

LOGE
Warum, du Kluger,
glückte dir's nicht?

MIME
Tarnhelm	Ach, der das Werk ich wirkte,
	den Zauber, der ihm entzuckt,
	den Zauber erriet ich nicht recht!
	Der das Werk mir riet
	und mir's entriss,
	der lehrte mich nun
	– doch leider zu spät! –
Alberich	welche List läg' in dem Helm:
	meinem Blick entschwand er,
	doch Schwielen dem Blinden
Grief	schlug unschaubar sein *Arm*.
	Das schuf ich mir Dummen
Ring	schön zu *Dank*!

LOGE
Gesteh, nicht leicht
gelingt der Fang.

WOTAN
Doch erliegt der Feind,
| *Loge* | hilft deine *List*. |

MIME
Mit eurem Gefrage,
wer seid denn ihr Fremde?

LOGE
Freunde dir;
von ihrer Not
| *Forge + Grief* | befrein wir der Niblungen Volk. |

Therefore I kept
the thing for myself,
to make its magic
rid me of Alberich's rule.
Perchance, yes, perchance
outwit him, and master the master,
subjecting his craft to my cunning.
The ring slips from his finger!
No, I will labour no longer!

He serves me, and I shall be free!

LOGE
And where, my wise one,
did you go wrong?

MIME
I only forged the helmet;
the magic that lurks inside,
that magic I cannot unlock.
What I forged for myself,
he took by force.
O, then I found out,
alas, far too late,
what a spell lived in the helm.
From my sight he vanished,
and I came to feel
his quite invisible fist;
and, sot that I am,
it serves me right!

LOGE [to Wotan]
Admit, not easy
is our task.

WOTAN
Yet the foe will fall,
thanks to your skill.

MIME
Have done with your prying!
Pray, strangers, who are you?

LOGE
Friends of yours.
We shall set free
the ill-fated Nibelung folk.

Mime's runaway tongue is his fatal flaw: he volunteers more information than is good for him. It is his garrulity which will, in *Siegfried*, procure his deserved demise.

This is an important question, which Mime should have asked at the outset.

Combined Forge and Grief motifs depict Nibelheim's sad toilers.

MIME

Nehmt euch in acht!

Alberich Alberich naht.

WOTAN

Forge + Grief Sein harren wir *hier.*

ALBERICH

Hieher! Dorthin!
Hehe! Hoho!
Träges Heer,
dort zu Hauf
schichtet den Hort!
Du da, hinauf!
Willst du voran?
Schmähliches Volk,
ab das Geschmeide!
Soll ich euch helfen?
Alles hieher!

He, wer ist dort?
Wer drang hier ein?
Mime! zu mir,
schäbiger Schuft!
Schwatzest du gar
mit dem schweifenden Paar?
Fort, du Fauler!
Willst du gleich schmieden und
  schaffen?

He, an die Arbeit!
Alle von hinnen!
Hurtig hinab!
Aus den neuen Schachten
schafft mir das Gold!
Euch grüsst die Geissel,
grabt ihr nicht rasch!
Dass keiner mir müssig,
bürge mir Mime,
sonst birgt er sich schwer
meiner Geissel Schwunge:
dass ich überall weile,
wo keiner mich wähnt,
das weiss er, dünkt mich, genau!

MIME [terrified, as he becomes aware of
Alberich's approach]
Be on your guard!
Alberich comes!

WOTAN [seating himself, with Loge
standing by his side]
We'll wait for him here.

ALBERICH [without his Tarnhelm now,
driving a crowd of Nibelungs before him;
they are laden with gold and silver which
they pile up in a hoard]
Come here! Go there!
Hehe! Hoho!
Lazy lot,
heap on heap
pile the hoard high!
Up with you there!
On with your work!
Barbarous brood,
hand me your harvest!
Shall I assist you?
Here with it all! [he notices Wotan and
Loge]
What have we here?
Who entered in?
Mime, come here,
you wretched rogue!
Prattling perchance
with this vagabond pair?
Off, you dawdler!
Back to your fiery furnace! [he drives
Mime away with his whip, then addresses
the Nibelung slaves]
Back to your labour!
Back to your burrows!
Hurry below!
In the new-made shafts,
go gather new gold!
This whip shall greet you,
if you go slow!
If any be idle,
Mime shall answer,
and then let him savour
my rod's caresses!
I go hither and yonder –
you will not know where,
as Mime learnt to his cost.

On Alberich's words 'pile the hoard
high' violins and violas play the
Forge motif, which now sounds
uncannily like the Rhinemaidens'
joyful 'Heiajaheia!'. Alberich is
aware, possibly with some regret, of
the origin of his power and what it
cost him.

	Zögert ihr noch?
Ring	Zaudert wohl gar?
Grief	Zittre und *zage*,
	gezähmtes Heer:
Gold's Dominion	rasch ge*horcht*
	des Ringes Herrn!

Was wollt ihr hier?

WOTAN
Von Nibelheim's nächt'gem Land
vernahmen wir neue Mär:

mächt'ge Wunder
wirke hier Alberich:
daran uns zu weiden,
Loge trieb uns Gäste die *Gier*.

ALBERICH
Nach Nibelheim
führt euch der Neid:
so kühne Gäste,
Loge glaubt, kenn ich *gut*.

LOGE
Kennst du mich gut,
kindischer Alb?
Nun sag: wer bin ich,
dass du so bellst?
Im kalten Loch
da kauernd du lagst,
wer gab dir Licht
und wärmende Lohe,
wenn Loge nie dir gelacht?
Was hülf' dir dein Schmieden,
Loge heizt' ich die Schmiede dir *nicht*?
Dir bin ich Vetter
und war dir Freund:
nicht fein drum dünkt mich dein
    Dank!

ALBERICH
Den Lichtalben
lacht jetzt Loge,
Loge der list'ge *Schelm*:
bist du Falscher ihr Freund,
wie mir Freund du einst warst,

Lingering still?
Dare to delay? [he kisses his ring and
holds it out threateningly]
Tremble in terror,
you harnessed horde,
subjects to
the ring's great lord! [they shriek and
scatter, while Alberich eyes Wotan and Loge
with suspicion]
What would you here?

WOTAN
Of Nibelheim's dark domain
strange stories have reached our
    ears:
daring deeds,
accomplished by Alberich!
We envy such wonders.
Welcome give to your guests!

ALBERICH
To Nibelheim
brings you your greed.
The likes of you, friends,
I've met before.

LOGE
Met us before,
ignorant imp?
Then say, who am I,
that you would growl?
In chilly caves
you fretted and froze;
who gave you light,
and who lit your fire-place?
I, Loge, smiled on you then!
No use was your furnace,
till I had heated the forge.
I am your kinsman,
I am your kind.
No warmer welcome for me?

ALBERICH
The Lichtalben
love their Loge,
that cunning rogue.
Are you friend to the gods,
as you once were to me?

As Alberich kisses the ring, its motif
sounds *pianissimo* in clarinet, cor
anglais, trumpet and bass trumpet –
a potent mixture, designed to
intimidate.

The ring's power depends on the
trepidation it inspires in its be-
holders. Without fear, it seems to be
ineffectual, as will be seen.

Wotan's excuse for his unrequested
arrival shows him, for once, as a
diplomat.

Loge's reminder is irrefutable. He
could argue that of all the gods he
alone is indispensible.

Lichtalben are light elves, in other
words the gods.

haha! mich freut's!
Von ihnen fürcht ich dann nichts.

LOGE
So denk ich, kannst du mir traun?

ALBERICH
Deiner Untreu trau ich,
nicht deiner Treu!
Doch getrost trotz ich euch allen!

LOGE
Loge Hohen *Mut*
verleiht deine Macht:
grimmig gross
wuchs dir die Kraft.

ALBERICH
Siehst du den Hort,
den mein Heer
dort mir gehäuft?

LOGE
Treasure So neidlichen sah ich noch nie.

ALBERICH
Das ist für heut
ein kärglich Häufchen:
kühn und mächtig
soll er künftig sich mehren.

WOTAN
Zu was doch frommt dir der Hort,
da freudlos Nibelheim,
und nichts für Schätze hier feil?

ALBERICH
Schätze zu schaffen
und Schätze zu bergen,
Treasure nützt mir Nibelheims *Nacht*;
doch mit dem Hort,
in der Höhle gehäuft,
Ring denk *ich* dann Wunder zu wirken:
die ganze Welt
Ring gewinn ich mit ihm zu eigen.

WOTAN
Wie beginnst du, Gütiger, das?

Haha! I'm glad!
Then I have nothing to fear!

LOGE
So trust me, I shall be true!

ALBERICH
I will trust your falsehood,
but not your truth.
I am safe, and I defy you!

One of Alberich's occasional flashes
of wit.

LOGE
See, what pride
your power confers!
See, what might
grows from your guile!

ALBERICH
Look at the hoard
that my slaves
heaped up for me!

LOGE
My envy is hard to contain.

ALBERICH
Just one day's work,
not much to boast of.
But in future
it will grow beyond measure.

WOTAN
How wasted, though, is your wealth
in joyless Nibelheim,
where gold finds nothing to buy.

Wotan's shrewd question meets
with a devastating reply.

ALBERICH
Wealth is created,
and wealth is entombed here,
deep in Nibelheim's night.
But with my hoard
which is heaped in the vaults,
I shall work marvellous wonders:
the whole wide world,
I swear, shall be mine for ever!

WOTAN
But my friend, how could that be
    done?

ALBERICH

Die in linder Lüfte Wehn
da oben ihr lebt,

Freia lacht und *liebt*
mit goldner Faust
euch Göttliche fang ich mir alle!

Liebe-Tragik Wie ich der *Liebe* abgesagt
alles, was lebt,

Freia soll ihr ent*sag*en!
Mit Golde gekirrt,
nach Gold nur sollt ihr noch
gieren.

Walhall Auf *wonn*igen Höhn
in seligem Weben
wiegt ihr euch;
den Schwarzalben
verachtet ihr ewigen Schwelger!
Habt acht! Habt acht!
Denn dient ihr Männer
erst meiner Macht,
eure schmucken Frau'n,
die mein Frein verschmäht,
sie zwingt zur Lust sich der Zwerg,

Liebe-Tragik *lacht* Liebe ihm nicht
Haha haha!

Treasure Habt ihr's gehört?
Habt acht!
Habt acht vor dem nächtlichen
Heer,
entsteigt des Niblungen Hort

Grief *Rhinegold* aus stummer *Tiefe zu* Tag!
Walhall

WOTAN

Vergeh, frevelnder Gauch!

ALBERICH

Was sagt der?

LOGE

Sei doch bei Sinnen!

Loge *Wen* doch fasste nicht Wunder
erfährt er Alberichs Werk?
Gelingt deiner herrlichen List,

Arrogance was mit dem Horte du heischest
den Mächtigsten muss ich dich
rühmen:
denn Mond und Stern'
und die strahlende Sonne,
sie auch dürfen nicht anders,

ALBERICH

You who breathe the balmy air,
aloft where you live,
love and laugh:
my golden fist
shall land me a shoal of immortals.
Once I foreswore delights of love.
Now let the world
prosper without it.
You gluttons for gold
shall thirst and hunger for gold
    now.
On heavenly heights
your easy abode,
your cradling clouds:
the Schwarzalbe,
you blacken him, blissful eternals!
Beware! Beware!
Your menfolk first
shall bow to my might,
then your winsome women,
– how they trifled with me! –
they all shall answer my lust,
though love be no more.
Haha haha!
You have been warned!
Beware!
Beware of my legions of night!

For soon the Nibelung gold
shall rise and ravish the world!

WOTAN
Begone, rascally rogue!

ALBERICH
What says he?

LOGE [to Wotan]
Control your anger! [to Alberich]
Who could see and not marvel
at mighty Alberich's art?
If only your art could achieve
all those golden ambitions,
then I would acclaim you
    almighty,
for moon and stars,
and the sun in its glory,
even they must be your minions,

Alberich's remembrance of his
potential for love – here expressed
by the Freia motif – still haunts him,
even at his most malignant.

Alberich, who has forsworn love, is
now able to purchase sexual gratifi-
cation. He has it both ways, like
Wotan – who seizes the ring for
pragmatic reasons, but then keeps it
for himself for expediency.

Wotan's occasional insensitivity
mars his negotiating powers. In
Scene 2 he insulted the giants; now
he does the same to Alberich. He
clearly needs the diplomatic Loge as
a minder.

Like a skilled lawyer, Loge always
sees all sides of an argument.
Where Wotan's judgment is fallible
– he has only one eye! – Loge pon-
ders all possibilities before presenting them to his client.

Alberich's lengthy monologue is a
terrifying forecast of a world con-
trolled by an unscrupulous dictator,
who will not hesitate to use his per-
nicious secret weapons. It makes
Wotan's pre-emptive strike
politically necessary, though morally
questionable.

Alberich quotes the Walhall motif, in
its original key of D flat major. He is
Wotan's alter ego, the 'Schwarz-
alberich' (Black Elf) to Wotan's
'Lichtalberich' (Light Elf).

The Liebe-Tragik motif lets Alberich
dwell regretfully on the first syllable
of 'Liebe'. He recalls what he for-
swore.

As unchallenged proprietor of Nibelheim's natural resources, Alberich
has an effective stranglehold on his
domain, which he is about to
extend to the rest of the world.

Walhall	*Arrogance*	dienen müssen sie *dir*
	Forge	Doch *wichtig* acht' ich vor allem,
		dass des Hortes Häufer,
		der Niblungen Heer,
		neidlos dir geneigt.
	Ring	Einen Reif führest du *kühn*,
	Forge	dem zagte zitternd dein Volk:
		doch wenn im Schlaf
		ein Dieb dich beschlich',
		den Ring schlau dir entriss',
		wie wahrtest du, Weiser, dich
	Loge	*dann*?

ALBERICH
Der Listigste dünkt sich Loge;
andre denkt er
immer sich dumm:

	Loge	*dass* sein ich bedürfte
		zu Rat und Dienst
		um harten Dank,
	Tarnhelm	das hörte der Dieb jetzt *gern*!

Den hehlenden Helm
ersann ich mir selbst;
der sorglichste Schmied,
Mime, musst' ihn mir schmieden:
schnell mich zu wandeln
nach meinem Wunsch,
die Gestalt mir zu tauschen,
taugt der Helm.
Niemand sieht mich,
wenn er mich sucht;
doch überall bin ich,
geborgen dem Blick.
So ohne Sorge
bin ich selbst sicher vor dir,

Arrogance	*Loge*	du fromm sorgender *Freund*!

LOGE
Vieles sah ich,
Seltsames fand ich:
doch solches Wunder
gewahrt' ich nie.
Dem Werk ohnegleichen
kann ich nicht glauben;
wäre dies eine möglich,
deine Macht dann währte ewig.

servants, slaves to your will.
Yet, weigh one thing above all
    things:
let your treasure troopers,
the Nibelung host,
never nurse ill will!
When your fist brandished the ring,
your folk would shudder and
    shake.
But, in your sleep
a thief might slip in,
and then ravish the ring.
Can prudence protect you from
    that?

ALBERICH
A slippery snake is Loge.
None as wise
and witty as he.
My cry for assistance,
for sly advice,
my hearty thanks,
that's what he would love to have.
This counterfeit cap,
devised by myself,
was craftily forged.
Mime made it to order.
I am myself,
and now I am not!
To assume any semblance,
serves the helm.
None can see me,
seek as he will;
but everywhere am I,
concealed from you all.
I am secure
and really quite out of your reach,
my kind, cousinly friend.

LOGE
Much I've met with,
many a marvel,
but such a marvel
I never saw.
Such limitless power!
None would believe it!
Were you to work such magic,
you would live and lord it for ever.

Loge considers the possibility of
Alberich conquering space: an
astonishing notion, since the nine-
teenth century was largely earth-
bound in vision and observance.

Alberich's contempt for Loge is
shown in the derisive acciaccaturas
(very short notes, squeezed in
rapidly before the principal notes)
on 'Der *Listig*ste *dünkt* sich *Log*e;
*and*re *denkt* er *im*mer sich dumm.'

ALBERICH
Meinst du, ich lüg'
und prahle wie Loge?

LOGE
Bis ich's geprüft,
bezweifl' ich, Zwerg, dein Wort.

ALBERICH

Forge Vor *Klug*heit bläht sich
zum Platzen der Blöde!
Nun plage dich Neid!
Bestimm, in welcher Gestalt
soll ich jach vor dir stehn?

LOGE
In welcher du willst:
nur mach vor Staunen mich
Tarnhelm *stumm*!

ALBERICH
'Riesen-Wurm
Dragon winde sich ringelnd!'

LOGE
Ohe! Ohe!
Schreckliche Schlange,
verschlinge mich nicht!
Schone Logen das Leben!

WOTAN
Hahaha! Hahaha!
Gut, Alberich!
Gut, du Arger!
Wie wuchs so rasch
zum riesigen Wurme der Zwerg!

ALBERICH
Hehe! ihr Klugen,
glaubt ihr mir nun?

LOGE
Mein Zittern mag dir's bezeugen.
Zur grossen Schlange
schufst du dich schnell:
weil ich's gewahrt,

ALBERICH
You think I lie
or bluster, like Loge.

LOGE
Show me some proof,
and then I will praise your art.

ALBERICH
Blown up with your brilliance,
you puff till you're bursting.
Then envy me now!
Decide and say in what shape
shall I promptly appear?

Alberich would have been well
advised to refrain from demonstrating the efficiency of the Tarnhelm.

LOGE
Whichever you will,
but strike me dumb with surprise!

ALBERICH [puts on the Tarnhelm]
'Dragon dread,
coiling and toiling!'
[Alberich disappears. A huge serpent raises
itself towards Loge and Wotan.]

The only appearance of the Dragon
motif in *Das Rheingold*. We shall
meet it again, in *Siegfried* and
Götterdämmerung.

LOGE
Ohe! Ohe!
Mightiest monster!
Have mercy on me!
Spare poor Loge, o spare me!

His alarming display of the Tarnhelm's power is a solemn moment.
Unfortunately, clumsy stagings can
turn this into a farce. Producers
should hire a professional magician
as a serpent- and toad-consultant.

WOTAN
Hahaha! Hahaha!
Good, Alberich!
Good, you rascal!
So fast! So fierce!
Transformed was the dwarf in a
    trice!

ALBERICH [reappears as himself]
Hehe! you shrewd ones,
now are you sure?

LOGE
My trembling tells its own story!
A mighty monster
grew in your place!
Now I have seen,

'My trembling tells its own story.'
Kettledrum and low strings tremble
in mock sympathy with Loge.

willig glaub ich dem *Wun*der.
Doch, wie du wuchsest,
kannst du auch winzig
und klein dich schaffen?
Das Klügste schien' mir das,
Gefahren schlau zu entfliehn:
das aber dünkt mich zu schwer!

ALBERICH
Zu schwer dir,
weil du zu dumm!
Wie klein soll ich sein?

LOGE
Dass die feinste Klinze dich
   fasse,
wo bang die Kröte sich birgt.

ALBERICH
Tarnhelm   Pah! nichts leichter!
Luge du her!
'Krumm und grau
krieche Kröte!'

LOGE
Dort die Kröte,
greife sie rasch!

ALBERICH

Ohe! Verflucht!
Ich bin gefangen!

LOGE
Halt ihn fest,
Grief   bis ich ihn band.

Nun schnell hinauf:
dort ist er unser.

Arrogance   Loge   Ring   Liebe-Tragik
Forge   Grief   Liebesnot

now I also believe it.
You can grow tall,
but can you grow tiny,
quite slight and slender?
How prudent that would be,
to hide from peril and surprise.
But, surely, that is too hard.

ALBERICH
Too hard, yes,
for such as you!
How small shall I be?

LOGE
That the tiniest crack will conceal
   you,
where toads might timidly hide.

ALBERICH
Nothing simpler!
Loge, look here! [puts on the Tarnhelm]
'Gaunt and grey,
toad, come creeping!'
[Alberich disappears. A toad comes crawling
towards Loge and Wotan.]

LOGE
Look, the toad there!
Capture it, quick! [Wotan stamps on the
toad. Loge catches it by the head and seizes
the Tarnhelm.]

ALBERICH [reappears as himself, writhing
under Wotan's foot]
Ohe! Accurst!
Now they have caught me!

LOGE
Hold him tight,
till he's trussed up! [ties his hands and
feet with a rope]
Let's go! Be quick!
Up with our quarry! [they drag
Alberich up, the way they came]

Puss in Boots goaded the ogre into
turning himself first into a lion and
then into a mouse. The cat then
pounced on him and devoured him.
Wagner probably knew the story.

The interaction of cor anglais with
three clarinets results in perfect
tone painting.

The scene ends with the Arrogance
motif's extended victory celebration.

Transition

Wotan and Loge have returned from Nibelheim with Alberich as their prisoner, just as Freia is the giants' hostage. Will Wotan ransom her with Alberich's gold? Will Loge have his way and see the gold returned to the Rhine? It is difficult to see Wotan making the correct choice. If he pays off the giants, he regains Freia but dupes the Rhinemaidens. But if he returns the gold to the Rhinemaidens, Freia will remain with the giants, and the gods will wither away. If he keeps the gold for himself, he may reign supreme, but he will also relinquish his position as giver and upholder of law.

Attempting to rule the world places the ruler on a slippery slope. He has to make compromises, he has to square his conscience, and he may have to go to war. Too late will he recognize that not he but Necessity rules all life. Wotan will learn this lesson in the course of the unfolding drama. But not just yet.

The Music: from Nibelheim to the Mountain Heights

As the gods abduct the fettered Alberich, woodwind and horns announce the Arrogance motif. The full orchestra rises in pitch and volume on the Loge motif, denoting the threesome's upward journey. Strings repeat the Ring motif thirteen times in succession, before the trombones sound their plaintive Liebe-Tragik motif. This is how Alberich views the world and, in particular, his own fate. Incessant Forge and Grief motifs accompany the travellers, played first by strings and tubas, then once again by the eighteen anvils. These are followed by the horns' melancholy Liebesnot motif. *Pianissimo* cellos and double basses remind Wotan, with the Giants motif, that he will soon have to decide whether to pay or to defraud Freia's captors. The next sequence of motifs are Walhall, Loge, Giants and Grief, before the minor version of Golden Apples, sighed by woodwind and horns, sends another appeal to Wotan's conscience. To compound the augury of doom, strings play the Grief motif, again and again, louder and louder. The woodwind's *fortissimo* Loge motifs are taken up by the strings, until the whole dismal journey ends with nine shrieked Grief motifs in strings and horns. The travellers have arrived on the mountain. Walhall looms on the horizon. So does Necessity.

Paul Kuen as Mime
surrounded by the Nibelungs,
Bayreuth 1950s

Wotan leads the gods into Walhall
on the rainbow bridge; lithograph
by Franz Stassen (1914)

Scene 4

Synopsis
Leitmotifs
Libretto

Scene 4: Story

Open Space on a Mountain Top

Wotan and Loge have arrived on the mountain height with their prisoner. Wotan demands Alberich's gold as his ransom. With the help of his magic ring, Alberich summons the Nibelungs, who appear with the golden treasure. When they depart Alberich asks for his freedom, but he is forced to surrender the Tarnhelm first. Wotan also demands the ring and, when Alberich refuses to part with it, he tears it from the dwarf's hand. Alberich then casts a spell on the ring, cursing it and all its future owners.

Alberich vanishes, and the other gods arrive to greet Wotan. The giants return with Freia, whose presence restores the gods' youthful appearance. To ransom Freia, the giants request sufficient gold to cover her up completely, so that she is hidden from their sight. Wotan is forced to surrender the Tarnhelm as well, but when Fasolt examines the piled-up treasure he can still see Freia's eyes. Fafner points to Wotan's ring, to stop up the chink. Wotan indignantly refuses. The giants renounce their proposed exchange, and are about to abduct Freia when Erda appears from below. She warns Wotan to yield the ring and to flee from its curse. She adds that the end of the gods is near, whereupon Wotan throws the ring upon the pile. The giants release Freia, and Alberich's curse is seen to work: Fafner kills his brother for the ring. Donner calls up a storm to clear the air, and Froh creates a rainbow bridge, for the gods to ascend into Walhall. The Sword motif gives notice of Wotan's bold plan to engender a descendant who, armed with Wotan's sword, shall secure the gods' survival. The Rhinemaidens are heard bewailing their lost gold, as the gods enter into Walhall. Loge, however, goes his own way.

Wotan, riveted by the sight of Walhall; illustration by Maxfield Parrish (1894)

Scene 4: Action

1. Wotan demands Alberich's ransom
2. Alberich summons the Nibelungs
3. Arrival of the hoard
4. Tarnhelm surrendered
5. Wotan demands the ring
6. Alberich as moralist
7. Wotan takes the ring from Alberich
8. Alberich's curse
9. Orchestra: Alberich disappears
10. A moment's repose
11. The giants demand Freia's ransom
12. Freia to be covered by the hoard
13. Setting of the stakes and building of the pile
14. Tarnhelm surrendered
15. Fasolt refuses to give up Freia
16. Fafner demands the ring
17. Wotan refuses to give up the ring
18. Erda's warning
19. Wotan surrenders the ring
20. Fafner kills Fasolt
21. Thunder and Rainbow
22. Wotan salutes Walhall
23. Wotan's sword conceived in his mind
24. The gods enter Walhall
25. The Rhinemaidens bewail their lost gold

Scene 4: Leitmotifs

The leitmotifs new to the scene follow in chronological order, together with the page number of first appearance.

Nibelungen Hate   p.148

Curse   p.148

Erda   p.160

Götterdämmerung   p.160

Thunder   p.168

Rainbow   p.168

Sword   p.168

Commentary on the Leitmotifs

Nibelungen Hate

A motif without melody, but full of menace. Upwards sweeping cellos are answered by an intricate syncopated rhythm on the clarinets. During Alberich's diatribe we hear it eighteen times in succession. This is designed to inspire fear or, since Wotan and Loge are gods, at least unease.

Curse

The previous motif lacked melody, the present one is without harmony. Alberich's voice alone pronounces its upwards arching course which then falls, dramatically, a whole octave, while the kettledrum plays a rapid tremolo, a forerunner of the trembling recipients of the curse. The motif is a near-inversion of the Ring motif.

Erda

This is a minor-key version of the Genesis motif: Erda is as old as the world itself. The motif rises from the ground, even as Erda ascends. Brass and eerie bassoons announce it at a sudden key change – Wagner's way of drawing our attention to an important moment.

Götterdämmerung

The motif is an inversion of the Genesis motif. Played one after the other, the music describes a full circle, a ring. There are no further appearances of this motif in either *Rheingold* or *Walküre*. It will next be heard in *Siegfried*.

Thunder

This motif shares its beginning, the rising fourth, with the Rhinegold, Sword and Rainbow motifs. It is first sung by Donner, then repeated by the horns, to Wagner's stage direction, 'He disappears in a dark thunder cloud, and we hear his hammer striking the rock, when a lightning flash darts through the cloud, followed by a violent thunderclap.' The brief Thunder motif expresses all this to perfection. It will be heard only once more, at the beginning of *Walküre*.

Rainbow

Not so much a motif as a descriptive musical phrase. Its wide-spanning arch represents the rainbow bridge leading to Walhall. The full orchestra, with six harps, is required for this passage. It is heard only once more, at the very end of *Rheingold*.

Sword

Psychologically, the Sword motif represents Wotan's attempt to cut through the Gordian knot of cause and effect, and thus to nullify Alberich's curse. Musically, it impresses immediately on account of its martial assertiveness, as the key changes to a bright C major, with trumpets heralding 'Wotan's great thought', the promise of an all-conquering sword for an unborn hero.

Donner clears the air with his
hammer; lithograph by Franz
Stassen (1914)

4. Szene

LOGE
Da, Vetter,
sitze du fest!
Luge, Liebster,
dort liegt die Welt,
die du Lungrer gewinnen dir
  willst:
welch Stellchen, sag,
Arrogance bestimmst du drin mir zum Stall?

ALBERICH
Schändlicher Schächer!
Du Schalk! Du Schelm!
Löse den Bast,
binde mich los,
den Frevel sonst büssest du
  Frecher!

WOTAN
Gefangen bist du,
fest mir gefesselt,
wie du die Welt,
was lebt und webt,
in deiner Gewalt schon wähntest,
in Banden liegst du vor mir.
Du Banger kannst es nicht leugnen!
Zu ledigen dich,
bedarf's nun der Lösung.

ALBERICH
Oh, ich Tropf,
ich träumender Tor!
Wie dumm traut' ich
dem diebischen Trug!
Furchtbare Rache
räche den Fehl!

After the full orchestral sound in
most of Scene 3, the orchestra is
now greatly reduced in volume and
numbers.

Scene 4

[Open space on a mountain top. The view is
shrouded in mist, as at the end of the second
scene.]

LOGE
Here, kinsman,
come and sit tight!
Look, beloved,
there lies the world
that was yours for the taking,
  you troll.
What corner, pray,
was set aside for my cell?

ALBERICH
Rascally robber!
You cheat! You rogue!
Loosen my bonds,
do let me go,
or else you shall pay for your
  pleasure!

WOTAN
My captive are you,
fast in my fetters,
just when the world
and all its wealth
was yours for one magic moment.
But here you kneel at my feet;
you, fellow, cannot deny it.
You want to be free?
Then pay for your freedom!

ALBERICH
I was dumb,
and duped by my dreams.
A fool, trapped by
their fraudulent tricks.
Fearful revenge
shall follow this wrong!

Having outwitted Alberich, Loge is
in flippant mood. Wagner directs,
'He snaps his fingers and dances
round him.'

LOGE
Soll Rache dir frommen,
vor allem rate dich frei:
dem gebundnen Manne
büsst kein Freier den Frevel.
Drum, sinnst du auf Rache,
rasch ohne Säumen
Arrogance   sorg um die *Lösung* zunächst!

ALBERICH
So heischt, was ihr begehrt!

WOTAN
Ring   Den Hort und dein helles Gold.

ALBERICH
Gieriges Gaunergezücht!
Doch behalt ich mir nur den Ring,
des Hortes entrat ich dann leicht:
denn von neuem gewonnen
und wonnig genährt
ist er bald durch des Ringes
    Gebot.
Eine Witzigung wär's,
die weise mich macht:
zu teuer nicht zahl ich die Zucht,
lass für die Lehre ich den Tand.

WOTAN
Erlegst du den Hort?

ALBERICH
Löst mir die Hand,
Ring   *Grief*   so ruf ich ihn her.
Gold's Dominion   *Forge*

Wohlan, die Niblungen
Treasure   rief ich mir nah:
ihrem Herrn gehorchend
hör ich den Hort
aus der Tiefe sie führen zu
    Tag.
Nun löst mich vom lästigen Band!

WOTAN
Forge + Grief + Treasure   Nicht eh'r, bis alles ge*zahlt.*

LOGE
Not dreaming of vengeance?
You'd better dream yourself free.
To a slave in fetters
free men owe no repayment.
So if you are plotting
vengeance, plot promptly:
let your ransom be rich!

ALBERICH
Go on! What must I give?

WOTAN
The hoard and your gleaming gold.

ALBERICH
Covetous cluster of crooks!
But, so long as I keep the ring,
the treasure will be no great loss.
It would soon be regained
and handsomely heaped,
through the magical spell of the
   ring.
It shall be a warning
to make me more wise.
This lesson will not have been lost:
gladly I give up all my gold.

WOTAN
Hand over the hoard!

ALBERICH
Loosen my hand!
I'll summon it here. [Loge unties
Alberich's right hand. Alberich kisses his
ring and murmurs a command.]
Behold, the Niblungen
answer my call.
I am still their master!
Hark to the hoard
being humped from below to the
   light!
Unbind now those tedious bonds!

WOTAN
I shall, but first pay my price! [the
Nibelungs ascend with the hoard]

The instantaneous arrival of the
hoard demonstrates the power of
the ring and strengthens Wotan's
resolution to deprive Alberich of this
potent weapon. At this moment
Wotan probably recalls Alberich's
earlier threat, 'Beware of my legions
of night! For soon the Nibelung gold
shall rise and ravish the world!'

Alberich's kiss is a dramatic repeti-
tion of his gesture in Scene 3, when
he commanded his slaves to 'Tremble in terror, you harnessed horde!',
and is reinforced by the same
music.

A triple motif illustrates the treasure
being carried up: the Forge motif
(cello), Grief (low woodwind) and
Treasure (trombone).

ALBERICH
O schändliche Schmach,
dass die scheuen Knechte
geknebelt selbst mich erschaun!
Dorthin geführt,
wie ich's befehl!
All zu Hauf
schichtet den Hort!
Helf ich euch Lahmen?
Hieher nicht gelugt!
Rasch da, rasch!
Dann rührt euch von hinnen:
Fort in die Schachten!
Weh euch, treff ich euch faul!

Gold's Dominion Auf den Fersen folg ich euch nach.

Gezahlt hab' ich:
nun lass mich ziehn!
Tarnhelm Und das *Helm*geschmeid,
das Loge dort hält,
das gebt mir nun gütlich zurück!

LOGE
Zur Busse gehört auch die Beute.

ALBERICH
Ring Ver*flucht*er Dieb!
Doch nur Geduld!
Der den alten mir schuf,
schafft einen andern:
noch halt' ich die Macht,
der Mime gehorcht.
Schlimm zwar ist's,
dem schlauen Feind
Tarnhelm zu lassen die listige Wehr!

Nun denn! Alberich
liess euch alles:
jetzt löst, ihr Bösen, das Band!

LOGE
Bist du befriedigt?
Lass ich ihn frei?

WOTAN
Ein goldner Ring
ragt dir am Finger:

ALBERICH
O scandalous shame!
That my fearful lackeys
should see their master's disgrace!
Carry it there,
as I command!
In a heap
pile up the hoard!
Dogs, shall I help you?
Don't dare look at me!
Hurry! Haste!
Be off now and leave us!
Back to your burrows!
Move those laggardly limbs,
and expect me hard on your heels!
[Alberich kisses his ring and stretches it
out. The Nibelungs quickly descend in
terror.]
Your gold, take it
and let me go.
And that helm of mine
which Loge still holds,
be good enough, give it to me.

LOGE [throws the Tarnhelm on the hoard]
That plunder is part of the ransom.

ALBERICH
Confounded thief!
Yet, wait awhile!
He who made the one,
makes me another.
Mine still is the might
which Mime obeys.
Sad it seems
that now my foe
should come by my cunning
    device.
Now then, Alberich
paid his ransom,
so free me, brutes, from my bonds.

LOGE [to Wotan]
Are you contented?
Shall he go free?

WOTAN
A golden ring
flames on your finger.

To equip the treasure, Wagner
bought forty-four items from a
Bayreuth coppersmith, such as oil
cans, funnels, buckets, kettles and
cake tins.

Alberich shudders at being seen as
a slave by his own slaves.

'Shall he go free?' asks Loge, avoid-
ing any mention of the ring which
Alberich still holds. Be it on Wotan's
conscience to propose the robbery.

hörst du, Alb?
Der, acht ich, gehört mit zum Hort.

ALBERICH
Der Ring?

WOTAN
Zu deiner Lösung
musst du ihn lassen.

ALBERICH
Das Leben – doch nicht den Ring!

WOTAN
Den Reif verlang ich:
mit dem Leben mach, was du
    willst.

ALBERICH
Lös' ich mir Leib und Leben,
den Ring auch muss ich mir lösen:
Hand und Haupt,
Aug und Ohr,
sind nicht mehr mein Eigen
als hier dieser rote Ring!

WOTAN
Dein Eigen nennst du den Ring?
Rasest du, schamloser Albe?
Nüchtern sag,
wem entnahmst du das Gold,
daraus du den schimmernden
    schufst?
War's dein Eigen,
was du Arger
der Wassertiefe entwandt?
Bei des *Rhein*es Töchtern
hole dir Rat,
ob ihr Gold sie
zu eigen dir gaben,
das du zum Ring dir geraubt.

ALBERICH
Schmähliche Tücke,
schändlicher Trug!
Wirfst du Schächer
die Schuld mir vor,
die dir so wonnig erwünscht?
Wie gern raubtest

Hear me, troll:
that also is part of the price.

ALBERICH
The ring?

WOTAN
You want your freedom.
Forfeit the ring then!

ALBERICH
My life, but never the ring!

WOTAN
The ring surrender!
For your life I care not at all.

ALBERICH
If you allow my life,
then the ring must also be granted.
Hand and head,
eye and ear,
they are my own birthright,
and so is this bright red ring!

WOTAN
That ring – your birthright indeed!
Brazen-faced, blustering Niblung!
Tell me, how
did you get that gold
which served for the radiant
    ring?
Did you own it,
when you ravished
the Rhinemaids' glittering gold?
Will those watery daughters
witness for you,
that they gave you
their gold as your birthright?
Marauding rogue, you're a thief!

ALBERICH
Mischievous baseness!
Monstrous deceit!
Do you damn me
for what I did?
How you must welcome the deed!
Confess, you would

Alberich is horror-struck when
Wotan demands the ring. Plucked
strings, *fortissimo*, punctuate his
frenzied 'The ring?' as he imagines
the ring being plucked from his
finger.

Without the ring my life is worth
nothing, declares Alberich. He is
quite right: has he not paid a price
for it which no other living creature
is prepared to pay?

du selbst dem Rheine das Gold,
war nur so leicht
die Kunst, es zu schmieden,
　erlangt?
Wie glückt' es nun
dir Gleissner zum Heil,
dass der Niblung ich
aus schmählicher Not,
in des Zornes Zwange,
den schrecklichen Zauber gewann,
des Werk nun lustig dir lacht?
Des Unseligen,
Angstversehrten
fluchfertige,
furchtbare Tat,
zu fürstlichem Tand
soll sie fröhlich dir taugen,
zur Freude dir frommen mein

Ring 　Fluch?
Hüte dich,
herrischer Gott! ·
Frevelte ich,
so frevelt' ich frei an mir:
doch an allem, was war,
ist und wird,
frevelst, Ewiger, du,
entreissest du frech mir den Ring!

WOTAN

Treaty 　*Her* den Ring!
Kein Recht an ihm
Rhinegold 　schwörst du schwatzend dir zu.

ALBERICH
Ha! Zertrümmert! Zerknickt!
Liebe-Tragik 　Der *Traur*igen traurigster Knecht!

WOTAN
Nun halt ich, was mich erhebt,
Ring 　der Mächtigen mächtigsten Herrn!

LOGE
Grief 　Ist er ge*löst*?

WOTAN
Bind ihn los!

have gladly stolen the gold,
had it not been
far harder to forge than to
   filch.
It serves your turn,
you treacherous god,
that the Niblung here,
in dire distress,
in a maddened moment,
has purchased a sinister skill:
its outcome smiles now on you!
My doomed, desperate,
panic-stricken,
curse-carrying,
deadliest deed –
a trifling affair
for a god's entertainment?
Shall bliss be your boon for my
   curse?
Guard yourself,
arrogant god!
If I have sinned,
my sins shall be mine alone;
but on all that shall be,
is and was,
falls your sin for all time,
if Wotan ravished the ring!

WOTAN
Mine the ring!
Not yours but mine!
Rant and rave as you will. [he seizes
Alberich and forces the ring from his finger]

ALBERICH
Ha! Defeated! Destroyed!
Of slaves the unhappiest slave!

WOTAN
I hold what makes me supreme:
of lords the omnipotent lord.

LOGE
Shall he go free?

WOTAN
Turn him loose!

Here the Rhinegold motif undergoes a terrible transformation,
as the woodwind distort and
dismantle it.

Now it is Wotan's turn to emulate
Alberich's ring-kissing ceremony.
But whereas on the two previous
occasions the Ring motif that
accompanied the gesture was
pianissimo, it now is *fortissimo*,
rapidly diminishing to *piano*:
Wotan's joy in the ring is to be
short-lived.

Wotan receives his second lecture in
ethics (the first was from Fasolt in
Scene 2). Alberich is as horrified as
was Fasolt before him when he per-
ceives the god's moral laxity.

Wotan demands the ring, as the
Treaty motif, representing his conscience, is played very quietly by
cellos and double basses.

Before and after Alberich's outburst
of 'Zertrümmert!' (defeated), woodwind and horns hint at the Brooding motif, which is to play an important part in *Siegfried*.

LOGE

Schlüpfe denn heim!
Keine Schlinge hält dich:

Nibelungen Hate   frei fahre dahin!

ALBERICH

Bin ich nun frei?
Wirklich frei?
So grüss' euch denn
meiner Freiheit erster Gruss!
Curse   *Wie* durch Fluch er mir geriet,
verflucht sei dieser Ring!
Gab sein Gold
mir Macht ohne Mass,
nun zeug' sein Zauber
Tod dem, der ihn trägt!
Ring   *Kein* Froher soll
seiner sich freun;
keinem Glücklichen lache
Nibelungen Hate   sein lichter Glanz!
Wer ihn besitzt,
den sehre die Sorge,
und wer ihn nicht hat,
den nage der Neid!
Jeder giere
nach seinem Gut,
doch keiner geniesse
mit Nutzen sein!
Ring   Ohne *Wuch*er hüt' ihn sein Herr,
doch den Würger zieh' er ihm
     zu!
Dem Tode verfallen,
fessle den Feigen die Furcht;
solang er lebt,
Grief   sterb' er lechzend da*hin*,
des Ringes Herr
als des Ringes Knecht:
bis in meiner Hand
den geraubten wieder ich
Grief   halte!
So segnet in höchster Not
der Nibelung seinen Ring!
Behalt ihn nun,
hüte ihn wohl,
Grief   meinem Fluch fliehest du *nicht*.

LOGE [to Alberich]
Slip away home!
Not a sling detains you.
See, now you are free!

ALBERICH
Now am I free? [with a desperate laugh]
Really free?
I greet you all
with my freedom's first salute.
As my curse got me the ring,
my curse go with it now!
As it gave me
measureless might,
so by its magic
each owner shall die!
No carefree man
be free of care;
it shall smile not on him
who believes his luck.
Having the ring
means having ill fortune,
and not to have it
means living in hell.
All shall covet
its potent craft,
but none shall it profit,
and prosper shall none!
It shall bring its guardian no gain,
for it dwells where murderers
    dwell.
Let death be his doom,
let fear be his undying friend,
and let his life
turn to lingering death:
the ring's great lord
as the ring's great slave;
till my gold returns,
till my hand shall hold what was
    stolen!
Thus, racked by defeat and doom,
the Niblung blesses his ring.
Now is it yours:
keep it with care!
But my curse none shall escape!
[he vanishes in the crevice, while the
vapours clear away]

The downward sweeping string
figure which illustrates Loge's unty-
ing of Alberich is reversed, a few
bars later, into an upward sweep,
where it forms the first half of the
Nibelungen Hate motif.

The full orchestra shrieks the Grief
motif at Alberich's parting maledic-
tion, warning Wotan to expect hard
times.

LOGE
Lauschtest du
seinem Liebesgruss?

Giants

WOTAN
Gönn ihm die geifernde Lust!

LOGE
Fasolt und Fafner
nahen von fern;

Golden Apples
Freia führen sie *her*.

FROH

Golden Apples
Sie *kehr*ten zurück.

DONNER
Willkommen, Bruder!

FRICKA

Nibelungen Hate
Bringst du gu*te* Kunde?

LOGE
Mit List und Gewalt
gelang das Werk:
dort liegt, was Freia löst.

DONNER
Aus der Riesen Haft
naht dort die Holde.

FROH
Wie liebliche Luft
wieder uns weht,
wonnig Gefühl
die Sinne erfüllt!

Liebe-Tragik
*Traur*ig ging es uns allen,
getrennt für immer von ihr,
die leidlos ewiger Jugend
jubelnde Lust uns verleiht.

FRICKA
Lieblichste Schwester,
süsseste Lust!

Giants
Bist du mir wieder gewonnen?

LOGE
Did you mark
his salute of love?

WOTAN
Grant him his venomous grudge.

LOGE
Fasolt and Fafner
come from afar.
Freia follows them here. [the air is
clear now, and Donner, Froh and Fricka
come hurrying forward]

FROH
The two have returned.

DONNER
You're welcome, brother!

FRICKA
Have you brought good tidings?

LOGE
By fraud and by force
the prize was won.
This gold sets Freia free.

DONNER
See the giants there!
Welcome, our fair one!

FROH
How sweetly the breeze
soothes us now;
happy the glow
that gladdens our hearts!
Bleak is life and past bearing,
when we are severed from her,
who dowers youth everlasting,
laughter and halcyon days. [Fasolt
and Fafner enter, with Freia between them.
The gods look young again, and Fricka
rushes towards Freia.]

FRICKA
Sweetest of sisters,
dearest delight!
Have you come home, and for ever?

Wotan, according to Wagner's stage
direction, is 'lost in contemplation
of the ring on his finger'. Having
eliminated Alberich, however, does
not rid him of Alberich's curse.
People may be silenced; their influ-
ence tends to live on.

The change of key to C major, and
the ascending violins playing 'very
tenderly', herald Freia's return. The
gods hardly notice the kettledrum's
insistent Giants motif, which lasts
for a full twenty-three bars.

Fricka's question about 'good tidings' is sung to the Nibelungen Hate
motif. Thus Loge's 'This gold sets
Freia free' really means 'Don't touch
it, it is contaminated'; in modern
terms, it is radioactive.

The rare sound of the harp gives
Froh's lyrical words an exquisite
luminosity.

FASOLT

Giants Halt! Nicht sie berührt!
Noch gehört sie *uns*.
Auf Riesenheims ragender Mark
rasteten wir:
mit treuem Mut
des Vertrages Pfand
pflegten wir.
So sehr mich's reut,
zurück doch bring ich's,
Troth er*legt* den Brüdern
die Lösung ihr.

WOTAN

Bereit liegt die Lösung:
des Goldes Mass
Crisis sei nun gütlich gemessen.

FASOLT

Das Weib zu missen,
Freia wisse, gemutet mich *weh*:
soll aus dem Sinn sie mir
  schwinden,
des Geschmeides Hort
häufet denn so,
dass meinem Blick
Liebe-Tragik die *Blüh*ende ganz er verdeck'!

WOTAN

So stellt das Mass
Freia   *Liebesnot* nach Freias Gestalt.
Giants   *Troth*

FAFNER

Gepflanzt sind die Pfähle
nach Pfandes Mass:
gehäuft nun füll es der Hort.

WOTAN

Liebesnot *Eilt* mit dem Werk:
widerlich ist mir's!

LOGE

Giants Hilf mir, Froh!

FASOLT [restrains Freia]
Hold! Further away!
She is not yet free.
On Riesenheim's towering rocks
we took our ease.
In loyal hands
we have held the pledge,
honouring her.
With keen regret
I now return her,
but first deliver
the ransom due!

WOTAN
The ransom lies ready:
the gold shall now
be right royally granted.

FASOLT
To part with Freia,
painfully saddens my soul.
That I may fairly forget
  her,
let the gold be heaped,
pile upon pile!
Totally hide
the heavenly maid from my sight!

WOTAN
Then gauge the gold
by Freia's fair shape.
[the giants have planted their staves in the
ground and place Freia in between]

Freia, Liebesnot, Giants, Troth: this
cluster of motifs tells its own story.

FAFNER
Our poles have been planted
to fit her form;
thus high the hoard must be
  heaped.

WOTAN
On with the work:
spare me this outrage!

LOGE
Help me, Froh!

Wotan's shamefaced repugnance,
'On with the work! Spare me this
outrage!', is underlined by the
Liebesnot motif. For one rare
moment we see the real Wotan,
whose dark dealings, however
necessary, can still make him blush.

FROH
Freias Schmach
Troth *Forge* eil ich zu enden.

FAFNER
Nicht so leicht
Giants *Forge* und locker gefügt!
Fest und dicht
Treasure füll er das Mass!

Hier lug ich noch durch:
verstopft mir die Lücken!

LOGE
Zurück, du Grober!
Greif mir nichts an!

FAFNER
Hieher! die Klinze verklemmt!

WOTAN
Liebesnot *Tief* in der Brust
brennt mir die Schmach.

FRICKA
Sieh, wie in Scham
Freia schmählich die Edle *steht*:
um Erlösung fleht
stumm der leidende Blick.
Böser Mann!
Giants + Forge Der Minnigen botest du *das*!

FAFNER
Noch mehr! Noch mehr!
Noch mehr hieher!

DONNER
Kaum halt ich mich:
schäumende Wut
weckt mir der schamlose Wicht!
Hieher, du Hund!
Willst du messen.
so miss dich selber mit mir!

FAFNER
Ruhig, Donner!
Rolle, wo's taugt:
hier nützt dein Rasseln dir nichts!

FROH
Freia's disgrace,
let it be ended! [Loge and Froh heap up
the hoard between the staves]

FAFNER
Not so light,
so light and so loose!
Firm and tight
fill up the gauge! [he stoops down to
look for holes]
I still can see through:
those holes must be hidden!

As Fafner demands more and still
more golden treasure, the Forge
and Giants motifs sound simultaneously. Fafner is creating his own
Nibelheim.

LOGE
Stand back, you savage!
Touch nothing here!

FAFNER
See there! That cleft must be
   closed!

WOTAN
Deep in my heart
burns her disgrace.

FRICKA
See where she stands,
purity put to shame.
For your help she hopes.
See her sorrowful gaze!
Wretched man,
it's you brought our fair one to this!

FAFNER
More! More!
Pile on some more!

DONNER
No more of this!
Furious rage
rouses this insolent rogue.
Come here, you hound!
Would you measure?
Then measure yourself against me!

FAFNER
Quiet, Donner!
Rumble elsewhere!
for here you bluster in vain.

DONNER
Nicht dich Schmähl'chen zu
   zerschmettern?

WOTAN
Troth   Friede *doch*!
Treasure + Forge   Schon dünkt mich Freia ver*deckt*.

LOGE
Golden Apples   Der Hort ging auf.

FAFNER
Noch schimmert mir Holdas Haar:
dort das Gewirk
wirf auf den Hort!

LOGE
Wie, auch den Helm?

FAFNER
Tarnhelm   *Hurt*ig her mit ihm!

WOTAN
Lass ihn denn fahren!

LOGE
So sind wir denn fertig.
Seid ihr zufrieden?

FASOLT
Freia, die schöne,
schau ich nicht mehr:
so ist sie gelöst?
Treasure   *Forge*   Muss ich sie lassen?
Freia   *Liebesnot*

Weh! Noch blitzt
ihr Blick zu mir her;
des Auges Stern
strahlt mich noch an:
Freia   durch eine *Spalt*e
Liebesnot   muss ich's erspähn!
Liebe-Tragik   Seh ich dies *wonn*ige
        Auge,
Liebe-Tragik   *Forge*   von dem *Weibe* lass ich nicht ab.

FAFNER
He! Euch rat ich,
verstopft mir die Ritze!

DONNER
Do you think I cannot crush you?

WOTAN
Gently, friend!
I find that Freia is hid.

LOGE
The gold gives out.

FAFNER
I still can see Holda's hair!
That odd thing, too,
toss on the hoard!

LOGE
Even the helm?

FAFNER
Quickly, here with it!

WOTAN
Well, let it go then.

LOGE [throws the Tarnhelm on the pile]
The matter is settled;
are we at peace now?

FASOLT
Freia, my fair one,
where are you now?
Bought back and redeemed?
Must I then lose you? [peering through
the pile]
Ah! her gaze
still gleams on me here!
Like stars, her eyes
dazzle me quite.
Yes, through this space
I look on their light.
Graceful those eyes as they greet
    me:
I must cling to the maiden divine!

FAFNER
Ha! I charge you
to stop up that cranny!

Even before Fafner's observation
about Freia's hair, muted horns
sound the Golden Apples motif,
pianissimo, predicting the looming
threat to the gods' continued
vitality.

In a memorable staging by Wagner's
grandson Wieland, the heaped-up
clumps of gold created the primitive
image of a female torso.

Fasolt is about to make his choice
between the gold and Freia. The
motifs of Freia and Liebesnot on the
oboe tell us what Fasolt sees and
feels.

LOGE
Nimmersatte! Seht ihr denn nicht,
ganz schwand uns der Hort?

FAFNER
Mitnichten, Freund!
An Wotans Finger
glänzt von Gold noch ein Ring,
den gebt, die Ritze zu füllen!

WOTAN
Wie? Diesen Ring?

LOGE
Joy Lasst euch *rat*en!
Den Rheintöchtern
gehört dies Gold:
ihnen gibt Wotan es wieder.

WOTAN
Was schwatzest du da?
Was schwer ich mir erbeutet,
Rhinegold ohne Bangen wahr ich's für *mich.*

LOGE
Schlimm dann steht's
um mein Versprechen,
das ich den Klagenden gab.

WOTAN
Dein Versprechen bindet mich
nicht:
Ring als Beute bleibt mir der *Reif.*

FAFNER
Doch hier zur Lösung
musst du ihn legen.

WOTAN
Fordert frech, was ihr wollt:
alles gewähr ich,
um alle Welt
doch nicht fahren lass ich den Ring!

FASOLT

Aus dann ist's,
beim Alten bleibt's:
nun folgt uns Freia für immer!

LOGE
Greedy grumbler, can you not see,
all gone is our gold.

FAFNER
Not quite, my friend!
On Wotan's finger
gleams a ring made of gold:
give that to fill up the crevice!

WOTAN
What? Give my ring?

LOGE
Let me tell you:
the Rhinemaidens
must have the ring,
and to them Wotan bestows it.

WOTAN
What nonsense is this?
I toiled to track this trophy:
it is mine by right of the chase.

LOGE
That goes badly
with the promise
I gave those sorrowful girls.

WOTAN
What you pledged, binds you, but
    not me.
My trophy! Mine is the ring!

FAFNER
But here as ransom
must it be rendered!

WOTAN
Ask for anything else,
all shall be granted,
but all the world
cannot make me part with this ring!

FASOLT [angrily pulls Freia out from
behind the treasure pile]
All is up!
Our treaty stands,
and we keep Freia for ever!

Now Wotan is made to feel what
Alberich felt in the same situation.
Again, plucked strings, *fortissimo*,
mark 'my ring?'. No man, giant or
dwarf will pluck it from his finger.
Only Necessity.

Loge's interjection sounds like
mischief-making. Yet, seeing every
side of the argument, he proposes
the morally correct action.

Fafner insists that 'as ransom must
it be rendered!' Horns play snatches
of the Ring motif, which now
sounds as though frozen in its
course. This foreshadows the fate of
the ring, and of the whole treasure.
Fafner is to make no use of them:
ring and treasure will be frozen
assets.

FREIA

Grief *Hilf*e! Hilfe!

FRICKA

Harter Gott,
gib ihnen nach!

FROH

Spare das Gold nicht!

DONNER

Spende den Ring doch!

WOTAN

Lasst mich in Ruh!

Ring   **Erda** Den Reif geb ich nicht.

ERDA

Weiche, Wotan, weiche!
Flieh des Ringes Fluch!
Rettungslos
dunklem Verderben
weiht dich sein Gewinn.

WOTAN

Wer bist du, mahnendes Weib?

ERDA

Erda Wie alles *war*, weiss ich;
wie alles wird,
wie alles sein wird,
seh ich auch:
der ew'gen Welt
Ur-Wala,
Erda mahnt deinen Mut.
Drei der Töchter,
ur-erschaffne,
gebar mein Schoss:
was ich sehe,
sagen dir nächtlich die

Nibelungen Hate   Nornen.
Doch höchste Gefahr
führt mich heut
selbst zu dir her.

Grief *Erda* *Hör*e! Höre! Höre!
Alles, was ist, endet.

Götterdämmerung Ein *düst*rer Tag

FREIA
Help me, help me!

FRICKA
Heartless god,
grant what they ask!

FROH
Pay the full ransom!

DONNER
Give them the ring too!

WOTAN
Leave me alone!
The ring is my all! [The stage is dark
again. Suddenly Erda appears in a bluish
light, rising from below.]

ERDA
Leave it, Wotan, leave it!
Flee the accursed ring!
Ruin, defeat
and ill fortune
live now in your ring.

WOTAN
Who are you, woman of doom?

ERDA
How all things were, know I;
how all things are,
how all things shall be,
I foresee.
The endless world's
Ur-Wala,
Erda, bids you beware.
Daughters three
created Erda,
before time was.
What my eyes see,
nightly you learn from the Norns'
    lips.
But danger most dire
drives me here,
goddess to god.
Hear me! Hear me! Hear me!
All that exists endeth.
A day of doom

Violins and violas plunge down,
fortissimo, with their incomplete
Ring motif, while cellos and double
basses rise in contrary motion; then
tubas and bassoons announce the
solemn Erda motif.

Erda as goddess of the earth was
Wagner's own concept, since his
sources do not mention any such
deity. He may have been motivated
by the Volva, a prophetess in the
Scandinavian Poetic Edda.

Wotan, says Erda, receives information from the Norns 'every night'.
Wagner seems to refer to Wotan's
dreams. In *Meistersinger* we hear
that 'our deepest wisdom here is oft
in dreams to us made clear.'

The Norns are Erda's daughters, and
represent past, present and future.
They weave the rope of destiny. We
shall meet them at the beginning of
Götterdämmerung.

Ring dämmert den Göttern:
dir rat ich, meide den Ring!

WOTAN
Erda Geheimnis-hehr
hallt mir dein Wort:
weile, dass mehr ich wisse!

ERDA
Ich warnte dich –
du weisst genug:
sinn in Sorg und Furcht!

WOTAN
Soll ich sorgen und fürchten –
dich muss ich fassen,
alles erfahren!

FRICKA
Was willst du, Wütender?

FROH
Halt ein, Wotan!
Scheue die Edle,
Erda achte ihr *Wort*!

DONNER
Hört, ihr Riesen!
Zurück und harret:
das Gold wird euch gegeben.

FREIA
Darf ich es hoffen?
Dünkt euch Holda
Erda   *Treaty* wirklich der Lösung wert?

WOTAN
Zu mir, Freia!
Du bist befreit.
Wiedergekauft
Liebe-Tragik *kehr* uns die Jugend zurück!

seeks the immortals.
Be counselled, flee from the ring!
[she begins to descend, and the bluish
light fades]

WOTAN
Elusive lore
flows from your lips.
Wait! Let me hear more wisdom!

ERDA
I've warned you now.
You know enough.
Weigh and dread my words!
[she disappears]

WOTAN
Must I ponder my peril,
then I command you,
tell me the whole truth! [he tries
to follow her down, but Froh and Fricka
restrain him]

FRICKA
What broods your maddened
   mind?

FROH
Have done, Wotan!
Erda is sacred:
heed what she says.

DONNER
Hear, you giants,
come back and listen!
The gold – Wotan will grant it.

FREIA
Dare I but hope it?
Does your Holda
merit such great amends? [all look
expectantly at Wotan who, at last,
brandishes his spear, to signal his decision]

WOTAN
To me, Freia!
Now you are free.
Purchased again,
youth everlasting, return!

Wotan bids for a second appoint-
ment with Fate, like Macbeth, who
sought another meeting with the
witches: 'I will tomorrow, and
betimes I will, to the Weird Sisters;
more shall they speak.'

Erda does not promise that giving
up the ring will delay the end of the
gods – whatever choice Wotan
makes, 'a day of doom seeks the
immortals.' In Wagner's prose sketch
to *Rheingold*, Erda had warned
Wotan to surrender the ring and
thereby save himself. But now he
can neither have his cake nor eat it.

Innocence *Freia* Ihr Riesen, nehmt euren Ring!

Giants *Forge*

FASOLT
Halt, du Gieriger!
Gönne mir auch was!
Redliche Teilung
taugt uns beiden.

FAFNER
Mehr an der Maid als am Gold
lag dir verliebtem Geck:
mit Müh zum Tausch
vermocht' ich dich Toren.
Ohne zu teilen,
hättest du Freia gefreit:
teil ich den Hort,
billig behalt ich
die grösste Hälfte für mich.

FASOLT
Schändlicher du!
Mir diesen Schimpf?
Euch ruf ich zu Richtern:
teilet nach Recht
Nibelungen Hate uns redlich den Hort!

LOGE
Den Hort lass ihn raffen:
Ring halte du nur auf den Ring!

FASOLT
Zurück, du Frecher!
Mein ist der Ring;
mir blieb er für Freias Blick.

FAFNER
Fort mit der Faust!
Der Ring ist mein!

FASOLT
Ich halt ihn, mir gehört er!

FAFNER
Crisis Halt ihn fest, dass er nicht fall'!

You giants, here is your ring! [He
throws it on the hoard, the giants release
Freia, and Fafner starts packing the gold in a
huge sack.]

FASOLT
Hold, you greedy one,
give me some also!
Measure for measure:
let us share it.

FAFNER
Yours was the girl, not the gold,
amorous, lovesick lad,
and grudgingly
you granted the barter.
Would you have shared her,
once you had Freia for bride?
Sharing the hoard?
Rightly I grasp now
the greater half for myself.

FASOLT
Infamous thief!
Mocking me thus?
You gods, be our judges:
duly divide
our share of the hoard!

LOGE [to Fasolt]
The hoard – let him have it.
Go for the golden ring!

FASOLT
Stand back, you blackguard!
Mine is the ring!
It lost me fair Freia's glance!
[seizes the ring]

FAFNER
Off with your fist!
The ring is mine!

FASOLT
I have it! I shall hold it!

FAFNER
Hold it fast, or it may fall!

The Nibelungen Hate motif accompanies Loge's advice to Fasolt, signifying that whoever obtains the ring also inherits its curse.

Fasolt calls upon the gods to give judgement. He still believes in the gods' superior ethical standing. He will not live to be undeceived.

This is the first of three instances of brothers fighting to the death over the ring. The second is between Alberich and Mime (in *Siegfried*), and the third between Gunther and Hagen (in *Götterdämmerung*).

Ring	Nun blinzle nach *Freias* Blick:
Curse	an den Reif rührst du nicht mehr!

WOTAN

	Furchtbar nun
Curse	erfind ich des Fluches Kraft!
Nibelungen Hate	

LOGE

	Was gleicht, Wotan,
	wohl deinem Glücke?
	Viel erwarb dir
	des Ringes Gewinn;
	dass er nun dir genommen,
Giants	nützt dir noch mehr:
	deine Feinde – sieh,
	fällen sich selbst
Ring	um das Gold, das du vergabst.

WOTAN

	Wie doch Bangen mich bindet!
Erda	Sorg und *Furcht*
	fesseln den Sinn;
	wie sie zu enden,
	lehre mich Erda:
	zu ihr muss ich hinab!

FRICKA

Enchantment	Wo *weilst* du, Wotan?
	Winkt dir nicht hold
Walhall	die hehre *Burg,*
	die des Gebieters
	gastlich bergend nun harrt?

WOTAN

Ring	Mit *bösem* Zoll
Curse	*zahlt'* ich den Bau!

DONNER

	Schwüles Gedünst
	schwebt in der Luft;
	lästig ist mir
	der trübe Druck:
	das bleiche Gewölk
	samml' ich zu blitzendem Wetter;

[he fells Fasolt and forces the ring from the dying man's hand]

So much for Freia's glance.
Not for you, rascal, this ring. [He puts the ring in his sack, together with the rest of the treasure. The gods stand in horrified silence.]

WOTAN
Fearful power
I find in the fatal curse.

LOGE
What luck, Wotan,
equals your fortune?
Ample riches
you got through the ring;
but the loss of its power
profits you more:
for your foes, behold,
fight to the death
for the gold you gave away.

WOTAN
How these portents oppress me!
Dread distress
strangles my mind.
How to disperse it,
none knows but Erda.
To her will I descend!

FRICKA
What would you, Wotan?
See, how it gleams,
your glorious fort,
facing its master,
offering roof and retreat!

WOTAN
But what a price
I had to pay!

DONNER
Sweltering haze
hovers around.
Hostile is
such oppressive heat.
I'll gather the clouds,
summon up lightning and thunder,

The grotesquely distorted Ring motif witnesses brother killing brother.

Thus dies an entirely blameless and honourable character, for love.

Loge congratulates Wotan to the accompaniment of the Nibelungen Hate motif. In other words, you have escaped the curse, but not Alberich's everlasting hate.

During the transition from Scene 1 to Scene 2 the Ring motif turned into the Walhall motif. Now the process is reversed, Walhall turning into Ring. Power has shifted.

das fegt den Himmel mir hell.

Thunder *He*da! Heda! Hedo!
Zu mir, du Gedüft!
Ihr Dünste, zu mir!
Donner, der Herr,
Thunder ruft euch zu Heer.
Auf des Hammers Schwung
schwebet herbei:
dunstig Gedämpf,
schwebend Gedüft!
Donner, der Herr,
ruft euch zu Heer!
Thunder *He*da! Heda! Hedo!

Bruder, hieher!
Weise der Brücke den Weg!
Rainbow

Froh
Zur Burg führt die Brücke,
leicht, doch fest eurem Fuss:
beschreitet kühn
Walhall ihren schrecklosen *Pfad*!

Wotan
Abendlich strahlt
der Sonne Auge;
in prächtiger Glut
prangt glänzend die Burg.
In des Morgens Scheine
mutig erschimmernd
lag sie herrenlos,
Ring hehr verlockend vor mir.
Von Morgen bis Abend
in Müh und Angst
Erda nicht wonnig ward sie gewonnen!
Es naht die Nacht:
vor ihrem Neid
Sword biete sie Bergung nun.
So grüss ich die Burg,
Sword sicher vor Bang und *Graun*.
Folge mir, Frau:
Walhall in Walhall wohne mit mir!

and clear the air for us all. [mounting
a rock and swinging his hammer]
Heda! Heda! Hedo!
To me, all you mists,
all vapours to me!
Donner, your lord,
summons his host.
As my hammer swings,
sail to my side!
Vapours and clouds,
hovering mists:
Donner, your lord,
summons his host.
Heda! Heda! Hedo! [He vanishes in a
thunder cloud. As he strikes the rock with
his hammer, lightning shoots from the cloud,
followed by thunder.]
Brother, to me!
Build us a bridge in the sky! [The
clouds lift. A rainbow bridge stretches from
Froh's and Donner's feet to the castle, which
glows in the sun.]

FROH
This bridge to the castle!
Light, yet firm to the foot.
Be not afraid:
without peril the path!

WOTAN
Evening has come,
the sun's eye sparkles.
How nobly glows
my castle sublime.
At the break of day
so bravely it swaggered,
waiting masterless,
calmly claiming its lord.
From dawn until sundown,
in gloom and grief,
no joy was there in the winning.
The night is near:
from its dark spite
now we shall be secure.
Hail, fortress, to you!
Nevermore dread and care.
Follow me, wife!
Let Walhall harbour us both!

As the gods contemplate their new
fortress home, six harps lend the
passage a much needed optimism.

An insubstantial thing is a rainbow
bridge. Will the citadel to which it
leads prove as incorporeal as its
approach route? But it should also
be remembered that a rainbow
symbolizes hope.

This moment, marked by the Sword
motif, is when Wotan resolves to
create a free hero: someone who is
not tainted by the god's pragmatic
dealings, one who carries neither
guilt nor responsibility. To him will
Wotan bequeath a conquering
sword. This hero shall, of his own
accord, right Wotan's wrongs.

FRICKA
Was deutet der Name?
Nie, dünkt mich, hört' ich ihn
    nennen.

WOTAN
Was, mächtig der Furcht,
mein Mut mir erfand,

Crisis wenn siegend es lebt,
Ring leg es den Sinn dir dar!

LOGE
Ihrem Ende eilen sie
Loge zu,
Ring *Loge* die so *stark* im Bestehen sich
    wähnen.
Fast schäm ich mich,
Loge mit ihnen zu *schaffen*;
zur leckenden Lohe
mich wieder zu wandeln,
spür ich lockende Lust.
Sie aufzuzehren,
die einst mich gezähmt,
statt mit den Blinden
blöd zu vergehn,
und wären es göttlichste
    Götter!
Nicht dumm dünkte mich das!
Bedenken will ich's:
Walhall wer weiss, was ich tu!

DIE DREI RHEINTÖCHTER
Joy *Rhein*gold! Rheingold!
Reines Gold!
Wie lauter und hell
Rhinegold leuchtetest hold du *uns*!
Um dich, du klares,
wir nun klagen.
Gebt uns das Gold!
O gebt uns das reine zurück!

WOTAN
Welch Klagen klingt zu mir her?

FRICKA
What name is this 'Walhall'?
I've never heard you pronounce it.

WOTAN
'Audacious and free' ...
'Conceived by my will' ...
'Victorious life' ...
That is what Walhall means. [the
gods begin to cross the rainbow bridge]

LOGE [looking back at the gods]
They are rushing straight to
   their end,
and they think they are gods ever
   lasting.
Ashamed am I
to sit at their table.
My passion for fire,
for flushes and flashes
will no more be denied.
To feast on those
who had fettered my force –
not to end blindly
with those blind gods –
those greatest, those gracious, most
   godlike –
I quite fancy my fate.
What next, I wonder?
Who knows what I'll do! [he is about
to follow the gods, as the song of the Rhinemaidens is heard from below]

THE THREE RHINEMAIDENS
Rhinegold! Rhinegold!
Guiltless gold!
How fair was your flame,
how you would cheer us all!
For your great glory
we are grieving.
Give us our gold,
o give back our guiltless gold!

WOTAN [pauses and turns to Loge]
What wailing comes from below?

The kettledrum's Crisis motif is to
sound relentlessly from here to the
end of the scene, providing another
hint – in addition to the flimsiness
of the rainbow bridge – that Walhall's impregnability may be an
illusion.

Loge's summing-up of the gods'
actions matches Puck's 'Lord, what
fools those mortals are!' in *A Mid-
summer Night's Dream*.

Loge's sardonic remarks contain
two poisoned barbs: 'My passion for
fire' is sung to the later Valkyrie
motif, and 'most godlike' to a snatch
of the Sword motif, with Loge's own
fire music flickering around. He is
already mocking Wotan's future
defences.

LOGE
Des Rheines Kinder
beklagen des Goldes Raub.

WOTAN
Verwünschte Nicker!
Walhall Wehre ihrem Ge*neck*!

LOGE
Ihr da im Wasser,
was weint ihr herauf?
Hört, was Wotan euch wünscht.
Glänzt nicht mehr
euch Mädchen das Gold,
in der Götter neuem Glanze
Arrogance sonnt euch selig fort*an*!

DIE DREI RHEINTÖCHTER
Joy *Rhein*gold! Rheingold!
Reines Gold!
O leuchtete noch
Rhinegold in der Tiefe dein lautrer Tand!
Traulich und treu
ist's nur in der Tiefe:
falsch und feig
Walhall *Sword* ist, was dort oben sich *freut*!

LOGE
The Rhine's fair daughters:
they weep for their stolen gold.

WOTAN
Accursed nixies!
Stop their harrowing howls!

LOGE [calling down into the valley]
You in the water!
Don't weep and don't wail!
Hear, what Wotan desires.
Bask no more
in forfeited gold,
but in Wotan's brave new glory
bask forever in bliss! [the gods laugh
and step on to the bridge]

THE THREE RHINEMAIDENS
Rhinegold! Rhinegold!
Guiltless gold!
Your lustre is lost,
never more will you daze the deep.
Grace and good faith
abide in the waters.
Wantons all,
you who inherit the world! [the gods
cross the bridge into Walhall]

The curtain falls.

Loge's teasing of the Rhinemaidens
can be regarded as a just reward for
their equally cruel teasing of
Alberich.

The glorious spectacle of the gods
entering Walhall is juxtaposed with
the Rhinemaidens' lament. The
spectator or listener must decide
where probity resides – above or
below?

'Alberich and his ring would have
been powerless to harm the gods
had they not themselves been sus-
ceptible to evil … anyone who has
followed the work sympathetically,
will entirely agree with Loge.'
(Wagner to August Röckel, 26
January 1854)

The day before he died, Wagner
played the Rhinemaidens' lament
and said, 'I am fond of those yearning creatures down below.'

'Believe me, nobody has ever composed in this manner. I think my
music must be frightening. It is a
morass of horrors and sublimities.'
(Wagner to Liszt, 15 January 1854)

Postscript

The end? On 14 January 1854 Wagner wrote 'Und weiter nichts?' ('And nothing else?') on the last page of his score sketch. Nothing else, except three more music dramas to complete *Der Ring des Nibelungen*: *Die Walküre*, *Siegfried* and *Götterdämmerung*. For a brief preview, here is what happens to the main characters:

WOTAN
Begets a son, Siegmund, with a mortal woman. To him he bequeathes the sword Nothung. He also begets a daughter, Brünnhilde, with Erda, and fathers a further eight daughters, the Valkyries.

FRICKA
Demands Siegmund's death, to punish him for his incestuous union with Sieglinde, his sister.

LOGE
Is called upon, at the end of the *Ring*, to destroy Walhall and the gods.

ALBERICH
Begets a son, Hagen, with a queen whose compliance he procures with gold.

MIME
Brings up Siegfried, orphan son of Siegmund and Sieglinde. Is killed by Siegfried.

FAFNER
Turns himself into a dragon and sleeps on his golden hoard, the Tarnhelm and the ring. Is slain by Siegfried.

ERDA
Condemns Wotan for withdrawing the godhead from Brünnhilde, their daughter.

RHINEMAIDENS
Having the gold restored to them, they survive the final cosmic catastrophe.

The Rhinemaidens tease
Alberich; illustration by
Knut Ekwall (1876)

History of *Das Rheingold*

Composition History

1851	November	Prose sketch completed
1852	March	Prose draft completed
1852	November	Verse draft completed
1853	November	Composition begun
1854	September	Composition completed

Performance History

1869	September	First performance: Royal Court Theatre, Munich
1876	August	First performance as part of *Ring* cycle: Festspielhaus, Bayreuth
1882	May	First British performance: Her Majesty's Theatre, London

Bibliography

Further Reading

A more complete bibliography is given in the author's companion volume in this series.

Benvenga, N. *Kingdom on the Rhine* (Harwich, 1983)

Blyth, A. *Wagner's 'Ring'* (London, 1980)

Burbridge, P. & Sutton, R., eds. *The Wagner Companion* (London, 1979)

Cooke, D. *I Saw the World End* (London, 1979)

Dahlhaus, C. *Richard Wagners Musikdramen* (Velber, 1971; Eng. trans., 1979)

Donington, R. *Wagner's 'Ring' and its Symbols* (London, 1963)

English National Opera Guide: *The Rhinegold* (London, 1985)

Kobbé, G. *Wagner's Ring of the Nibelung* (New York, 1897)

Lee, M. O. *Wagner's 'Ring'* (New York, 1990)

Leroy, L. A. *Wagner's Music Drama of the Ring* (London, 1925)

Magee, E. *Richard Wagner and the Nibelungs* (Oxford, 1990)

Mander R. & Mitchenson, J. *The Wagner Compendium* (London, 1977)

Millington, B., ed. *The Wagner Compendium* (London, 1992)

Newman, E. *Wagner Nights* (London, 1949)

Osborne, C. *The Complete Operas of Richard Wagner* (London, 1990)

Porges, H. *Die Bühnenproben zu den Bayreuther Festspielen des Jahres 1876* (Bayreuth, 1881–96; Eng. trans., 1983, as *Wagner Rehearsing the Ring*)

Porter, A., trans. *Richard Wagner: The Ring* (London, 1976)

Shaw, G. B. *The Perfect Wagnerite* (London, 1898, 4/1923/repr. 1972)

Skelton, G. *Wagner at Bayreuth* (London, 1976)

Spencer, S., trans. *Wagner's Ring of the Nibelung* (London, 1993)

Spotts, F. *Bayreuth, A History of the Wagner Festival* (New Haven, 1994)

Weston, J. L. *The Legends of the Wagner Dramas* (London, 1896)

Discography

Three recommended performances. An extended discography can be found in the companion volume.

1953
Clemens Krauss
Bayreuth Festival Orchestra
Wotan: H. Hotter
Alberich: G. Neidlinger
Loge: E. Witte
Fricka: I. Malaniuk
Mime: P. Kuen
Erda: M. von Ilosvay
Fafner: J. Greindl
Fasolt: L. Weber

An altogther magnificent issue, and a benchmark for the rest of the century. The orchestral playing is superb, and Hans Hotter's Wotan and Gustav Neidlinger's Alberich are still unsurpassed.
FOYER 15CF2011 (Mono)

1958
Georg Solti
Vienna Philharmonic
Wotan: G. London
Alberich: G. Neidlinger
Loge: S. Svanholm
Fricka: K. Flagstad
Mime: P. Kuen
Erda: J. Madeira
Fafner: K. Böhme
Fasolt: W. Kreppel

Lush strings, gorgeous brass, passionate conducting and Kirsten Flagstad's golden-toned Fricka, who makes this a First Lady's set.
DECCA 4141012 DH3

1993
Christoph von Dohnányi
Cleveland Orchestra
Wotan: R. Hale
Alberich: F.-J. Kapellmann
Loge: K. Begley
Fricka: H. Schwarz
Mime: P. Schreier
Erda: E. Zaremba
Fafner: W. Fink
Fasolt: J.-H. Rootering

Dohnányi proves himself, at this first attempt, an inspired, energetic and mature Wagnerian. He obtains magnificent playing from the Cleveland magicians, and his cast does him proud: we get top performances from gods, dwarfs and giants (apart from a slightly underpowered Fafner). The new Alberich is Franz-Josef Kapellmann. Make a note of this name – he will go very, very far. To cast Kim Begley as Loge was a stroke of genius: he is sensational. Nearing the end of his distinguished career, Peter Schreier presents a Mime that will be almost impossible to follow. Robert Hale's Wotan is superb, both in beauty of tone and in the way he invests the god with that elusive mixture of grandeur and melancholy. Technically, this is a state-of-the-art recording.
DECCA 443690-2 DH02

Videography

There are four performances of *Das Rheingold* on video. The companion volume gives details of the other dramas of the cycle.

Place	Bayreuth	Munich	New York	Bayreuth
Orchestra	Festival	Bavarian State	Met. Opera	Festival
Conductor	P. Boulez	W. Sawallisch	J. Levine	D. Barenboim
Producer	P. Chéreau	N. Lehnhoff	O. Schenk	H. Kupfer
Year	1980	1989	1990	1992
Video	Philips 07040i/2/3/4 3PHE2	EMI MVX9 91275-3	DG 072 418/19/20/21 3GH2	Teldec 4509 91123-3
Laserdisc	070 401-4 1PHE2/3	LDX9 91275-1	072 418-21 1GH2/3/3	4509 91122/3-6 and 94193/4-6

WOTAN	D. McIntyre	R. Hale	J. Morris	J. Tomlinson
FRICKA	H. Schwarz	M. Lipovsek	C. Ludwig	L. Finnie
LOGE	H. Zednik	R. Tear	S. Jerusalem	G. Clark
MIME	H. Pampuch	H. Pampuch	H. Zednik	H. Pampuch
ALBERICH	H. Becht	E. Wlaschiha	E. Wlaschiha	G. von Kannen
FREIA	C. Reppel	N. Gustavson	M. Häggander	E. Johansson
FROH	S. Jerusalem	J. Hopferwieser	M. Baker	K. Schreibmayer
DONNER	M. Egel	F. Cerny	A. Held	B. Brinkmann
ERDA	O. Wenkel	H. Schwarz	B. Svendén	B. Svendén
FASOLT	M. Salminen	J. Rootering	J. Rootering	M. Hölle
FAFNER	F. Hübner	K. Moll	M. Salminen	P. Kang
WOGLINDE	N. Sharp	J. Kaufmann	K. Erickson	H. Leidland
WELLGUNDE	I. Gramatzki	A. M. Blasi	D. Kesling	A. Küttenbaum
FLOSSHILDE	M. Schiml	B. Calm	M. Parsons	J. Turner

Leitmotifs of *Das Rheingold*

All the leitmotifs of the opera are listed below, in alphabetical order.

Alberich

Arrogance

Crisis

Curse

Dragon

Enchantment

Erda

Forge

Freia

Genesis

Giants

Golden Apples

Gold's Dominion

Grief

Götterdämmerung

Innocence

Joy

Liebe-Tragik

Liebesnot

Loge

Nibelungen Hate

Rainbow

Rhinegold

Ring

Sword

Tarnhelm

Thunder

Treasure

Treaty

Troth

Walhall

Photographic Acknowledgements

AKG London: 14, 50, 53, 100, 129, 130, 137
Bayreuther Festspiele GmbH/Raub: 49
Mary Evans Picture Library: 12, 97, 101, 132, 175
Mary Evans/Arthur Rackham Collection: 2, 52, 98